PARADISE
A Roadway to Heaven

LIVING LIFE
IN ETERNAL GRACE

PARADISE
A Roadway to Heaven

LIVING LIFE
IN ETERNAL GRACE

COMPILED BY

Robert C. Mussehl

_____

Cover design by Misook Chung and Mi Ae Lipe.
Text design by Mi Ae Lipe, What Now Design, www.whatnowdesign.com.

Cover illustrations and floral art by Susan Gaber.
Colorizing by Mi Ae Lipe.

Printed and bound in the USA by DigiCopy, Inc.,
Seattle, Washington.

To contact the author by email:
bobmussehl@earthlink.net

This book is available through
Elliott Bay Book Company
("Seattle's Best Bookstore," Reader's Choice,
Seattle Magazine, December 2006)
101 South Main Street, Seattle, WA 98104
206-624-6600
www.elliottbaybook.com

First Edition
ISBN: 1-4276-0209-3
Library of Congress: 2006935110

To God, from whom all grace and all blessings flow,
I profusely thank!

To God's human family on earth,
I pray for peace, prosperity, justice, and freedom.

SPECIAL STATEMENT
FATHER ROBERT F. DRINAN, S.J.

This unique volume contains some one hundred striking excerpts from the Qur'an, Muhammad, Rumi, Jesus, and the Bible. There are also beautiful quotations, poetry, and affirmations from Robert C. Mussehl and others.

The excerpts show dramatically that the Muslim religion is Abrahamic and that it concurs in the realization of Judaism and Christianity that God has intervened in history and has revealed Himself. Keep this book close to you. Read and pray over its contents. It will revive your belief in Heaven. It will bring you understanding, peace, and love.

— The Honorable Robert F. Drinan, S.J., Washington, D.C., November 2006

Father Robert F. Drinan, S.J., was formerly Dean of Boston College Law School (1956 to 1970) and served with great distinction in the U.S. Congress for ten years, from 1970 to 1980. (Because of religious responsibilities, Drinan did not seek reelection for a sixth term of office). Drinan, a Democrat from Massachusetts, was the first to introduce a resolution in Congress calling for the impeachment of President Richard Nixon. During his term of office as a member of the House Judiciary Committee, Drinan became an acknowledged American hero (and personal hero of Robert Mussehl) for his integral and most successful role, along with the Honorable Barbara Jordan, in the Watergate hearings, which ultimately led to President Nixon's resignation in August, 1974, over the Watergate scandal.

A Jesuit Catholic priest, Drinan was honored on numerous occasions (including the highest honor awarded by the American Bar Association, the ABA Medal) for his exceptional service and leadership in many human rights issues and civil rights advancements, as well as his lifelong dedication to creating a just and peaceful society. The ABA Medal is rarely awarded, and for only the most exceptional contributions from lawyers or judges. In 2004, this rare award was enthusiastically presented by the first African-American ABA president, Dennis Archer, who applauded Father Drinan's amazing legal accomplishments and for his lifelong, passionate protection of human rights for *all* people.

From 2003 to 2004 Father Drinan served on the Board of Directors of the ABA Center for Human Rights. He was a past chair of *both* the ABA Family Law Section and the ABA Section of Individual Rights and Responsibilities. Father Drinan is the author of numerous articles and eleven books, including *Can God and Caesar Co-Exist? Balancing Religious Freedom & International Law* and *The Mobilization of Shame: A World View of Human Rights*. Father Drinan was a law professor since 1981 at Georgetown Law Center in Washington, D.C. until his recent death. He was awarded honorary doctoral degrees by twenty-two colleges and universities. On May 10, 2006, Father Drinan was presented the Congressional Distinguished Service Award by the then Speaker of the House, Dennis Hastert, and the then House Minority Leader, Nancy Pelosi, on behalf of the U.S. House of Representatives. *[Sadly, Father Drinan died January 28, 2007, at the age of 86. Our big loss is Heaven's big gain. Father Drinan brought nobility and honor to the Catholic priesthood and to the legal profession. His ethical and moral presence will be sorely missed. He will always be an inspiration to all of us for the attainment of justice and peace for all. — Mussehl.]*

READERS' ACCLAIM

This collection of diverse verses is a wonderful testimony to the message of unity, and our belonging to a future heavenly home we all long to know and arrive at!

Robert has woven a beautiful tapestry from the threads of truth that will texture whatever path one is walking. Anyone would definitely feel included when reading this most meaningful and gorgeous anthology!

Read and share this uplifting, spiritual book. It will bring you much joy, peace, and hope! It is the perfect gift!

— Tia Bailey

In today's chaotic society, this book offers a quick way to refocus ourselves to the ultimate question every civilization has been asking: "What is our purpose being here?"

Mr. Mussehl offers an instant rejuvenation to our psychological, emotional, and spiritual healing through various philosophies, religions, and cultural references that are directly linked with this utmost important question for humanity. **Furthermore, this book clearly demonstrates that there is a God who has ultimate authority over everything!** *Paradise: A Roadway to Heaven answers the importance of reconciliation among us, regardless of which religion we follow!*

This spiritually fulfilling book offers hope, serenity, and love to everyone who reads it! Offer it to your friends, relatives, and loved ones to share a spiritually fulfilling journey. If we all follow the spiritual message offered by Paradise, we will all experience a much kinder society where everyone respects and loves one another as planned by GOD.

— Ryan M. Kang

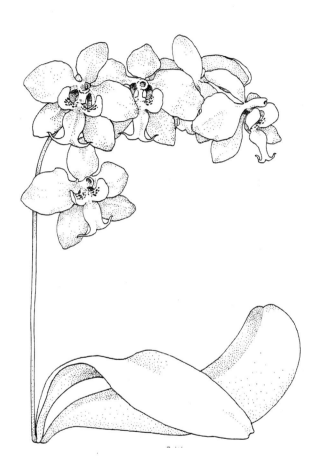

CONTENTS

FOREWORD

The soul needs beauty like the body needs food and shelter. Paradise *provides that beauty in abundance. People who have lived close to God are so filled with the beauty of Creation that all they can do is spill it over into their words.*

This wonderful book is a collection of some of the most beautiful words I've read in a long time. Pick any page, read it, breathe it in, and you will feel better.

The world is blessed that Robert is sharing this anthology with everyone.

— Reverend Dr. Kathianne Lewis

Kathianne Lewis currently serves as Senior Minister at the Center for Spiritual Living in Seattle. Lewis speaks nationally and is a featured columnist in the internationally distributed *Science of Mind* magazine. She is an author who inspires the greater Seattle community through her TV program, "Spiritual Living with Kathianne Lewis."

Robert Mussehl's Paradise *is a compilation which offers inspiration and solace for a troubled planet. Its selections are both familiar and inspirational. Its blend of contributions from the three major Western religions demonstrates the universality of faith. I was struck by the commonality of the three religions, beginning with the basic teaching from the Torah, "That which is hateful to you, do not unto others," as proclaimed by Rabbi Hillel; the Christian Golden Rule, "Do to others as you would have them do to you"; and the statement by Muhammad, "You are believers when you want for your brother, sister, and neighbor what you want for yourself."*

Robert shows us the continuing vitality of the common faith with his own observations.

— Phillip H. Ginsberg

Phillip H. Ginsberg is a Seattle attorney who has litigated cases involving racial injustice and police standards. He cofounded Human Rights for Bosnia and Save Darfur Washington State; he is also a past trustee and teacher at Temple Beth Am in Seattle. Ginsberg served as the president of the Board of the Defender Association from 2000 to 2005 and is a past president of the Seattle International District Rotary Club.

In the name of God, most Gracious, most Merciful: I have had the honor and pleasure of reading this wonderful anthology of beautiful quotations and would like to call it "a bouquet of flowers." Reading this book proves that different faith-traditions have the same idea of ONE God, and all want to live in peace and happiness. The Qur'anic and Hadith (sayings of Muhammad [peace be upon him]) quotations are from sound and accurate translations and capture the spirit of the advice quite appropriately, indeed! I shall be glad to gift and recommend this excellent work to friends and strangers alike, without any reservation at all! I enthusiastically recommend this beautiful book for all Muslims, Christians, Jews, Hindus, Buddhists, and other spiritually-minded people who love God and want to receive and feel His eternal love!

— Imam Sheikh Mohammad Joban

Mohammad Joban has been the imam for the Islamic Center of Olympia in Lacey, Washington, since 1990. Joban is also the president of the Imam Fatwa Committee and the current chaplain for all state penitentiaries in western Washington. Originally from Indonesia, Imam Joban holds a B.S. and M.S. in Usul Al-Din (Fundamentals of Religion) from Al-Azhar University in Egypt. On March 7, 2006, at the opening session and Benediction prayer for the Washington State House of Representatives, Joban's prayer for the House members, and for all of us, included the following: *"We pray that God guides the hearts of all good people of all faiths to see what we have in common, and pray that God makes us a stronger community and nation."*

Had he come along at a different time or resided on another side of the planet or chosen an alternate profession, Robert Mussehl might have been there for the Resurrection of Christ, sat in on the Paris peace talks, or put a definitive plan on the table for solving the never-ending Middle East crisis.

Instead he has attempted to bring the world together in this collection of spiritual wisdom that borrows from a wide range of religion, philosophy, and pop culture.

If you didn't feel happy, enlightened, or at peace with your surroundings when you opened this book, you did when you closed it.

— Dan Raley, Reporter, *Seattle Post-Intelligencer*

As I write these words, my mother-in-law, a person very dear to my wife and me for over sixty years, is near death at the astounding age of 112. In talking with her about what lies ahead, I told her that a Presbyterian minister who lost his wife to cancer called death "the great adventure that all of us will one day experience." Her answer: "I believe that is a good way to describe it!"

Those who keep this volume close at hand can prepare themselves joyfully for that great adventure! It can provide instant refreshment. Alfred Lord Tennyson asked us to approach death "sustained and soothed by an unfaltering trust." This precious volume will help every reader secure that trust; one can savor it for a minute or an hour.

— The Honorable Paul Findley

Paul Findley, a genuinely courageous American hero, served with great distinction in the U.S. Congress for twenty-two years and was the first of its members to propose normal diplomatic relations with China. A Republican from Illinois, he also wrote legislation that summons U.S. universities to challenge world hunger.

In 1976, Vice-President Nelson Rockefeller presented Paul Findley with the Estes Kefauver Memorial Award for promoting international federation. In 1977, Findley was awarded the Elijah Parish Lovejoy Award, which recognizes dual commitment to both individual freedom and freedom of the press. In 1978, Paul Findley was awarded the Order of Merit, the Commander's Cross, the highest civilian award of the Federal Republic of Germany, for his leadership regarding international human rights. In 1986, Findley received the Human Rights Award by the International Organization for All Forms of Racial Discrimination. In 2000, Findley received the Malcolm X Human Rights Award by the American Muslim Alliance in recognition for his extensive, long-term work and commitment to improve interfaith relations. He was also the recipient in 2000 of the Islamic Community Award by the Council on American-Islamic Relations for his leadership to eliminate all forms of racial and religious discrimination in the U.S. and the world.

Five colleges and universities have awarded Findley honorary doctorate degrees, including Illinois College, where he was a Phi Beta Kappa honors graduate. Findley is a cofounder of the Council for the National Interest, a Washington advocacy group, and author of several books, including *Silent No More: Confronting America's False Images of Islam; A. Lincoln: The Crucible of Congress;* and *They Dare To Speak Out,* the last of which sold over 300,000 copies.

PREFACE

Is there a Paradise? This is a question I have asked myself many times. What is the proof? Where is the evidence? I decided to do some personal research into this subject and wanted to share my discoveries, insights, affirmations, and poetry with others who are also looking for answers about our immortality, and the continuity and quality of life.

Our world needs healing from the political and religious strife that is all too constant today. Regardless of what religion and spiritual thinking we practice, we are all attempting to find peace and happiness in our lives. I hope that *Paradise* will inspire people of all religions to better understand and forgive one another, to be tolerant, and to concentrate on their common links to their faith in God. All caring human beings are called by God and their conscience to promote unity in diversity. We must all use the profound interfaith power of love, hope, justice, and kindness in forging this unity. Love transcends politics and cultural differences; love overrides fear, pettiness, and even hate.

Keep *Paradise* near you and make this exquisite book of wisdom and knowledge your constant traveling companion. At home, you will want to place this visually and spiritually beautiful book on your nightstand or coffee table for an instant supply of spiritual energy, hope, and peace!

To help readers better understand the verses of the Bible, Qur'an, *Bhagavad Gita*, and other religious scripture, I have modernized their language while retaining their true meaning. For example, I have removed some archaic words such as "thy," "thou," and "verily," as well as eliminated some gender-prejudiced references and other antiquated expressions. I thank you for understanding that my intent in providing this simple, less-cumbersome language is to make this book more reader-friendly.

The inclusion of verses from many sources along with those of the Q'uran in this book is to show the universal similarities among the various religions of the world. The intention is to promote a diversity of religious thinking and tolerance, which is much needed in our modern world.

Two other items of note: It is Islamic tradition that every mention of a prophet's name is followed with the phrase "peace be upon him," so this blessing appears after the names of Abraham, Jesus, Muhammad, and other prophets (peace be upon them). Also, instead of using the more customary Arabic "Allah" in the Islamic references, the term "God" is universally used throughout this book, regardless of the religion.

Ten percent of the net profits from sales of this book will be donated to causes benefiting the poverty-stricken and hungry of the world, especially at-risk children and orphans.

I hope and pray that you enjoy this offering and that you profit materially, peacefully, lovingly, and spiritually! God bless each of you — *always!*

— Robert C. Mussehl

ACKNOWLEDGEMENTS

My mother, Clara Cecelia Mussehl, who died in 2001 at age ninety-six, is my hero. She inspired me with her virtuous life and devotion to God and her family. My desire is to live a life that would make her happy with my choices and behavior, and would honor her life! I feel deeply grateful that God gave me a mother who loved me without condition and whose spiritual wisdom will always be with me. God bless *every* mother. God bless *every* parent! God bless *every* child! God bless *every* person on this earth!

I wish to especially thank Joanne Hendrickson and her husband Sharmarke Yusuf for their inspiring contributions to this book, Professor Sheikh Imam Ismail Ahmad for his scholarly expertise and guidance, and Nelda Danz, Rena Szirmai, Ian (Ibrahim) Clapp, Esq., and Kamran Salahuddin for their excellent proofreading and most helpful suggestions.

I also thank Zaid Abdul-Aziz* (Don Smith), Dr. Islamuddin Wardak, Mi Ae Lipe, Misook Chung (my talented and artistic wife), and everyone else who expressed their honest opinions and excellent suggestions for greatly improving this book.

— Robert C. Mussehl

---

* Zaid's own spiritual journey and autobiographical book, **Darkness to Sunlight,** *which I enthusiastically recommend, inspired the tribute to Rosa Parks on page 7. I am deeply grateful to Zaid for his inspirational message and his reminder of her incredible courage. (His book is available from Amazon.com and the Elliott Bay Book Co. [www.elliottbaybook.com, or 206-624-6600]).*

GRACEFUL
TRAVELS

Let There Be Justice and Peace for All
Let Freedom Reign!

We understand it still that
there is no easy road to freedom.

We know it well that none of us
acting alone can achieve success.

Let there be justice for all.

Let there be peace for all.

Let there be work, bread, water, and salt for all.

Let each know that for each
the body, the mind, and the soul
have been freed to fulfill themselves.

Let freedom reign.

— Nelson Mandela —
Inaugural address, upon becoming President of the Republic of South Africa
May 10, 1994

God's Plan Is Rooted in Love

God is Love.

God's plan for creation can be only rooted in Love!

Every saint who has penetrated to the core

of reality has testified

that a divine universal plan exists

and that it is beautiful

and full of Joy!

— *Swami Paramahansa Yogananda* —
Autobiography of a Yogi
Chapter 48

Seek Wisdom for Self-Harmony

Men and women who have faith have wisdom,
who live in self-harmony, whose faith is life,
and they who find wisdom, soon find the peace supreme.

But they who have no faith and no wisdom,
and whose souls are in doubt, are lost.
For neither this world, nor the world to come,
nor joy is ever for the person who doubts.

They who make pure their works,
who watch over their souls,
and who by wisdom destroy their doubts,
are free from the bondage of selfish work.

Kill, therefore, with the sword of wisdom,
the doubt born of ignorance that lies in your heart.
Be one in self-harmony ...
arise, great warrior, arise.

— *The Bhagavad Gita* —

Goodness Brings Rewards

Be really whole
and all things will come to you.

— *Lao-Tzu* —

You Are the One

Be the change you wish to see in the world.

— *Mahatma Gandhi* —

Thanks to God for Sending Us Rosa Parks

Rosa Parks (1913 to 2005) is an American hero and role model.
Heroes deeply inspire us in our travels in life.
Rosa was a pioneer for civil rights and social justice.

On December 1, 1955, in Montgomery, Alabama,
Rosa Parks rode a bus that was segregated by law at that time.
This law forced her and all other
African-Americans to sit only in the rear of
the bus and also to give up their seats to white persons.

Rosa refused to abide by these unjust segregation laws.
She was then arrested and fined for violating
this city ordinance, directly resulting
in the 1956 U.S. Supreme Court ruling that
Alabama's bus segregation laws were unconstitutional.

An inspirational hero to freedom-loving people everywhere,
Rosa Parks possessed an immense courage that later
sparked other successful challenges to racial segregation.

For instance, Dr. Martin Luther King, Jr. felt personally
moved and inspired by her courageous, noble actions
and lifelong commitment to advancing
human rights for *all* persons.

— *Robert C. Mussehl* —

Fatiha
The Opening Chapter and Verse of the Qur'an
Praise Be to God — The Cherisher and Sustainer of the Worlds

In the name of God,
most Gracious, most Merciful,
praise be to God,
the Cherisher and Sustainer of the worlds.

Most Generous, most Merciful,
Master of the Day of Judgment.

You alone do we worship, and Your aid do we seek.
Show us the straight way,
the way of those upon whom You, God Almighty,
have bestowed Your peace,
and not of those who have earned
Your wrath and gone astray.

— The Qur'an —
Chapter I (1), Verses 1–7

The Unity of Humankind
God Created Us from a Single Soul!
(The Family of Earth)

O humankind!
We created you from a single soul,
male and female, and made you into nations and tribes,
so that you may come to know one another.
Truly, the most honored of you in God's sight
is the greatest of you in piety.

God is knowing, all-aware.

— The Qur'an —
Chapter XLIX (49), Verse 13

Love Is the Answer — Love One Another

A new command I give you:
Love one another.

As I have loved you,
so you must love one another.

By this all people will know
that you are my disciples,
if you love one another.

— Jesus —
(Peace be upon him)
The Bible, John, Chapter 13, Verses 34–35

Promote Love

Love all religions and all nations.
Recognize and accept all religions
as paths leading humanity to the same destination.
All of them teach love and compassion,
humility, and forbearance.

Promote love, sympathy, and compassion toward all beings.
God is present in every one of them,
and it is your duty to revere God in each of them.

There is only one caste, the caste of humanity.
There is only one religion, the religion of love.
There is only one language, the language of the heart.
There is only one God and God is omnipresent.

— *Sai Baba* —

Spread the Compassion of Christ

Christ has no body now on earth but yours.
No hands but yours.
No feet but yours.

Yours are the eyes
through which Christ's compassion
looks out on the world.

Yours are the feet
with which Christ is
to go about doing good.

Yours are the hands
with which Christ is
to bless us now.

— *St. Teresa of Avila* —

Good Character Counts the Most

I have a dream today.
My dream is that little black boys
and little black girls
will join hands with little white boys
and little white girls,
and walk together as sisters and brothers. . . .

And our children will be judged
not by the color of their skin
but by the content of their character.

— Dr. Martin Luther King, Jr. —
"I Have a Dream" Speech
August 28, 1968

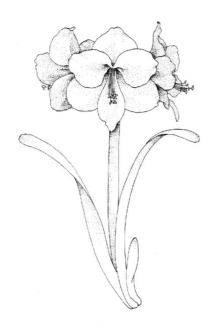

Be Kind and Caring

Kind, caring, and friendly people
have a wonderful and magical way
of making a difference in the life
of each person they meet.

— Robert C. Mussehl —

God Loves Unity in Diversity

Behold how good and how pleasant
it is for brethren
to dwell together in unity!

— The Bible —
Psalms, Chapter 133, Verse 1

We All Must Fight Injustice
and Promote Justice for All

Injustice anywhere is a threat to justice everywhere.

— Dr. Martin Luther King, Jr. —

How Can I Be Happy?

Develop an attitude of gratitude
and your happiness will increase immeasurably.

Gratitude opens our hearts to joy and love.

Gratitude humanizes us and connects us
to each other and to God.

— Robert C. Mussehl —

We Have Choices

You have brains in your head.

You have feet in your shoes.

You can steer yourself any direction you choose.

— Dr. Seuss —

Forgive Yourself

In the past we may have made many mistakes.

It is useless to worry about those things now.

Strive to shape the future;

that is what you must do.

— Ammachi —

I Believe Love Can Overcome Hate

I believe in the supreme worth of the individual
and that person's right to life, liberty,
and the pursuit of happiness.

I believe that every right implies a responsibility;
every opportunity, an obligation; every possession, a duty.

I believe that the law was made for humankind,
and that government is the servant of the people
and not their master.

I believe in the dignity of labor, whether with head or hand;
that the world owes no person a living,
but that it owes every person an opportunity to make a living.

I believe that thrift is essential to well-ordered living
and that economy is a prime requisite
of a sound financial structure,
whether in government, business, or personal affairs.

I believe that truth and justice are fundamental
to an enduring social order.

I believe in the sacredness of a promise,
that people's words should be as good as their bond;
that character — not wealth or power or position —
is of supreme worth.

I believe that the rendering of useful service
is the common duty of humanity,
and that only in the purifying fire of sacrifice
is the dross of selfishness consumed
and the greatness of the human soul set free.

I believe in an all-wise and all-loving God,
named by whatever name,
and that the individual's
highest fulfillment, greatest happiness,
and widest usefulness are to be found
in living in harmony with God's will.

I believe that love is the
greatest thing in the world;
that it alone can overcome hate;
that right can and will
triumph over might.

— *John D. Rockefeller, Jr.* —

Live with an Open Heart

Let me offer you this practice.
See all things with love, as a part of you.

For example: a flower.
Touch it with your love,
not just visually, but experientially.
Breathe in its aroma; it is part of you.
See its beauty; that is who you are.
Touch its softness; that is your softness.
Feel the strength of its roots.
That is your strength.
You would not see that flower
if it were not already a part of you.

Ultimately, your greatest teacher
is to live with an open heart.

— Pat Rodegast & Judith Stanton —
Emmanuel's Book: A Manual For Living Comfortably in the Cosmos

Sleep with God
Sleep All Night with God's Love and Protection!

How sad that night has fallen
and we've all separated.
Happy is the one
whose companion at night is God.

— *Rumi* —

Sleep in Peace, Grace, and Purity

Lie down on your right side,
after making ablution, and silently pray to God:

✳ Dear God, I have surrendered myself to You.

✳ I entrust every aspect of my life to You!

✳ There is no refuge or haven anywhere,
except refuge with You, and haven with You!

✳ I believe in Your word which You have
revealed and I believe in Your prophets
whom You have sent.

— *Muhammad* —
(Peace be upon him)

A Healthy Body Is Important
for Each of Us

The soul could never aspire to reach salvation,
unless it was able to have the support and cooperation
of the physical body.

The body is as important as the soul.
So by knowing the technique of tending and
nourishing the body well, I not only tended and
nourished the body, but the soul too.

But then I saw God within.
The body, I realized, is the Lord's temple;
and so I began preserving it with care infinite.

— *Thirumoolar* —

Smile!
A Warm Smile Is a Good Deed!

A cheerful heart is good medicine.

— The Bible —
Proverbs, Chapter 17, Verse 22

Share Your Joy

You have in your safekeeping
the soul of every person
you have ever smiled at.

— Pir Vilayat Inayat Khan —

God Is Bliss

Many flowers bloom on a tree
which sheds all its leaves.
On other trees
flowers bloom only here and there.

When we are totally free
from negative tendencies
such as selfishness, ego, and jealousy,
we will attain the vision of God.

Even if all beings in the world loved us,
we would not experience an iota
of the bliss we feel
from a moment's taste
of the Love of God.

So great is the bliss we feel from God's love
that there is nothing to
compare with it.

— *Ammachi* —

Be Tolerant!
We All Belong to God!

Let the different faiths exist.
Let them flourish.

Let the glory of God be sung
in all languages
and a variety of tunes.

That should be the ideal.

Respect differences between the faiths
and recognize them as valid.

— *Sai Baba* —

Remember God
Zikr Means the Remembrance of God
Practice Zikr Often for Peace and Comfort

In the remembrance of God,
hearts find rest and satisfaction.

— The Qur'an —
Chapter XIII (13), Verse 28

Zikr
God Will Bless and Reward Those Souls Who Remember God!

Remember God,
and God will remember you.

— The Qur'an —
Chapter II (2), Verse 152

There Is No God But God

God, there is no God but God,
the living, the self-sustaining.

— The Qur'an —
Chapter II (2), Verse 255

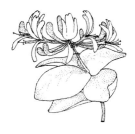

God Will Remove Our Sins

As for those who believe and do good deeds,
and believe what is revealed to Muhammad
— peace be upon him —
(and revealed to all of the prophets of God),
God will remove from them their sins
and improve their condition.

— The Qur'an —
Chapter XLVII (47), Verse 2

Do Your Best

When we do the best we can,
we never know what miracle is wrought in life,
or in the life of another.

— *Helen Adams Keller* —

God Is Love. Love Is God.

Love is God,
not merely as the noblest sentiment of a poet
but as an aphorism of eternal truth.

— *Swami Sri Yukteswar* —
The Holy Science
Chapter 4

Think of the Power of Words
Seek Education — Seek Knowledge — Knowledge Is Power!

* Choose carefully what you read.

* Keep good books close to you.

* Always think of the power of words.

* Make your library and your dictionary your best friends!

* Words are superb communication vehicles.

* Read for love, beauty, and your soul.

* Everything we read affects our thoughts and actions.

* Read for fun and adventure!

* Read inspirational books!

* Read to exercise your brain.

* Seek knowledge. Knowledge is power.

* Power brings you your dreams!

* Knowledge brings wisdom and peace.

* Peace frees the soul to sing and dance!

* Education opens golden doors of opportunity!

— Robert C. Mussehl —

Be Generous to the Orphans and the Needy

Righteousness is not that you merely
turn your faces to the East or the West;
rather, the righteous are those
who believe in God, and the Last Day,
and the Angels, and the Books, and the Messengers;
who give of material gifts out of love for God,
to relatives and to orphans, to the needy,
to the traveler, to those who ask,
and for the freeing of slaves;
who are steadfast in prayer and practice regular charity;
who fulfill the promises which they have made;
and are firm and patient in pain (or suffering)
and adversity and throughout all times of stress.

Such are the people of truth, the God-fearing.

— *The Qur'an* —
Chapter II (2), Verse 177

God Is the Most Pure

God is the King, the Most Pure,
the Perfect Peace, the Trustworthy,
the Safeguard, the Almighty,
the Compeller, the Supremely Great.

— The Qur'an —
Chapter LIX (59), Verse 23

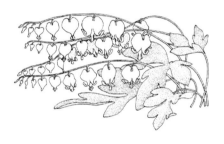

Reject False Gods

Anyone who rejects false gods and believes in God
has grasped the firmest Handhold,
which will never give way.
God is all-hearing, all-knowing.

— The Qur'an —
Chapter II (2), Verse 256

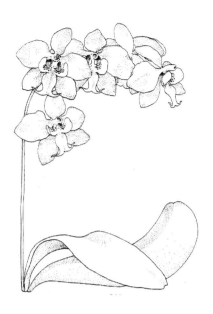

Be Humble

That which, when opposed,
seeks to assert itself, is ego.

When the ego dissolves,
then and there the soul becomes
possessor of all qualities —
the absolute.

— Thakur —

Give Charity Everyday

Charity is prescribed for each descendant
of Adam (peace be upon him) on every day the sun rises.

The doors of goodness are many:

* ✳ enjoining good,

* ✳ forbidding evil,

* ✳ removing harm from the road,

* ✳ listening to the deaf
  until you understand them,

* ✳ leading the blind,

* ✳ guiding one to the object
  of his or her need,

* ✳ hurrying with the strength of
  one's legs to one in sorrow
  who is asking for help,

* ✳ and supporting the feeble
  with the strength of one's arms —

all these are charity prescribed for you.

— *Muhammad* —
(Peace be upon him)

The Wonderful Lawlessness

Late in the winter
my heart is still a rose in bloom.

Late in the summer
I still have snow-covered peaks upon my back
where we can play and slide.

At night I need no candle or lamp,
for my soul has forever awakened

to there being just the reality of light
and the wonderful lawlessness of God.

Late in the winter I need no heat,
for I have entered the infinite fire.

Come, build a sled,
find a grand hill within my verse —

You and I and God
should play there more often
upon a peak such as Hafiz

That the Beloved has carved so well.

— Hafiz —

An Expression of Wisdom

If we are aware that a compassionate understanding
of others creates trust, then something changes.

If we understand that ignorance is the source of all conflict,
and if we strive to dissolve it, keeping silent
when words are superfluous, then something changes.

If we understand that knowledge without wisdom
leads to the death of the soul, then something changes.

If we realize that being angry or arguing with someone,
regardless of who may be at fault, is an impulsive reaction
through which we blame rather than understand,
and if we understand even those whom we blame,
then something changes.

If we practice the language of friendship,
and if we try to contribute to the well-being of everyone,
then something changes.

If we try to promote a path of inner realization,
without any desire to convince, then something changes.

If we set aside that which separates and
emphasize that which unites, then something changes.

If we abandon the desire for results and
do what must be done at each moment,
then something changes.

If we are aware that virtue demands submission
to the laws of life, and not to our own rules or ethics,
then something changes.

If we are faithful to what we are in our essence
and thereby act with discernment, then something changes.

If we accept that any search for security,
although an understandable desire, opposes
freedom of the soul, the Omega Point of Evolution,
then something changes.

If we are aware that fear,
experienced by the creature in all of us,
veils the aspiration of our inner being,
whose essence is divine, then everything changes.

And we witness the miracle that spirit can accomplish.

— *Frédéric Lionel* —

Pray for God's Forgiveness

When the help of God comes
and victory is achieved,
and the Prophet (peace be upon him)
sees people enter God's religion in crowds,
then celebrate the praises of our Lord,
and pray for God's forgiveness,
for God is oft-returning in grace and mercy.

— The Qur'an —
Chapter CX (110), Verses 1–3

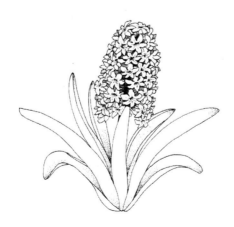

Counsel Each Other

By time men and women
are at a loss except for those:

* ✳ who have faith;

* ✳ who do righteous deeds;

* ✳ who counsel each other of truth;

* ✳ and who counsel each other
  of patience and constancy.

— The Qur'an —
Chapter CIII (103), Verses 1–3

God Is Incomparable

God is the One and Only,
the Self-sufficient,
upon Whom everything depends.

God begets not,
nor is God begotten,
and nothing can be
compared to God.

— The Qur'an —
Chapter CXII (112), Verses 1–4

God Has Power Over Everything

To God belongs all
that is in the heavens and on earth.

Whether you show what is
in your minds or conceal it,
God calls you to account for it.

God forgives whom God pleases,
and punishes whom God pleases,
for God has power over all things.

— The Qur'an —
Chapter II (2), Verse 284

We Must Forgive Deeply

Forgiveness is not the comfortable,
often somewhat superior "I forgive you" that comes
so easily to human lips when emotions have cooled.

Things are then smoothed over but the resentment
descends into the unconscious together
with a hidden condition that the
"forgiven" injury shall not be repeated.

The ultimate experience of forgiveness
brings a change of heart, a "metanoia" of the spirit,
after which every seeming injury, injustice, rejection
— past, present, or future — every so-called blow of fate,
becomes, as it were, an essential note in the music of God,
however discordant it may sound to our superficial hearing.

And the experience excludes nothing —
which means that in this moment of forgiveness
all one's own sins and weaknesses are included,
being at the same time both remembered and known
as the essential darkness
which has revealed to us the light.

— Helen M. Luke —

God Is the Supreme Artist

Blue paints the canvas,
Emerald green mountains below,
I the beholder above the earth and snow.

Feet are grounded even though not on solid ground,
Mind in the present while flying through clouds.
The earth is like a map waiting to unfold,
Following a destination, a path, a story not yet told.

Blue paints the canvas,
Opening the soul, the earth our divine mother,
Carries the wind where it needs to go.

Patterns make a weave all on their own,
Pieces ignite like a puzzle, golden soft tone,
Desolate spaces bury roots deep within,
Silver streaks of branches brushing against the earth's skin.

Blue paints the canvas that I am in.

— *Anonymous* —

Seek Happiness

I believe that the very purpose
of our life is to seek happiness.
That is clear.

Whether one believes in religion or not,
whether one believes in this religion or that religion,
we all are seeking something better in life.

So, I think the very motion
of our life is towards happiness.

— The Dalai Lama —
The Art of Happiness

Commitment

Commitment is what transforms
a promise into a reality.
It is the words that speak boldly
of your intentions …
and the actions that speak
louder than words.

It is making time when there is none …
and coming through —
time after time, year after year.

Commitment is the stuff character is made of;
that is, the power to change the face of things.
And it is the daily triumph
of integrity over skepticism.

— Anonymous —

We Are All Connected

At the heart of each of us,
whatever our imperfections,
there exists a silent pulse of perfect rhythm,
a complex of wave forms and resonances,
which is absolutely individual and unique,
and yet which connects us to
everything in the universe.

— *George Burr Leonard* —

The Guest House

This being human is a guest house,
every morning a new arrival.

A joy, a depression, a meanness,
some momentary awareness comes
as an unexpected visitor.

Welcome and entertain them all!
Even if they are a crowd of sorrows
who violently sweep your house
empty of its furniture,
still, treat each guest honorably.
God may be clearing you out for some new delight.

The dark thought, the shame, the malice —
meet them at the door laughing,
and invite them in.

Be grateful for whoever comes,
because each has been sent
as a guide from beyond.

— Rumi —

God's Plan Is Better

Not my will but thine, be done.

— Jesus —
(Peace be upon him)
The Bible, Luke, Chapter 22, Verse 42

Who Is God?

God is love;
and those that dwelleth in love
dwelleth in God,
and God in them.

— Jesus —
(Peace be upon him)
The Bible, I John, Chapter 4, Verse 16

Love Always Perseveres

* Love is patient.

* Love is kind.

* Love does not envy.

* Love does not boast.

* Love is not proud.

* Love is not rude.

* Love is not self-seeking.

* Love is not easily angered.

* Love keeps no record of wrongs.

* Love does not delight in evil.

* Love rejoices in truth.

* Love always protects.

* Love always trusts.

* Love always has hope.

* Love always perseveres.

* Love never fails.

— The Bible —
1 Corinthians, Chapter 13, Verses 4–8

Build Your Relationship with God

New existence overcoming the past.
It hurts to love, but that is what makes us grow.

We need love for inspiration
and higher self-consciousness.

Time and time again,
we take that step into the unknown,
wondering where this love will take us.

Only begin to truly love yourself
and you will begin to see
that the world can mean so much more.

Build a relationship with God
and true love will appear!

— *Anonymous* —

Love Yourself

One should love and nourish
each part of one's being:
the physical, vital, emotional, mental,
intellectual, and spiritual. . . .
Loving oneself is the very basis of yoga.

It allows one to love others
and ultimately to love God.

— *Marshall Govindan* —
Babaji and the 18 Siddha Kriya Yoga Tradition

Be a True and Sincere Believer

You are believers when you want
for your brother, sister, and neighbor
what you want for yourself.

— Muhammad —
(Peace be upon him)

Be Moderate in Your Religious Practices

Religion is easy, and whoever overburdens themselves
in their religion will not be able
to continue in that way.

So you should not be extremists, but try to be near
to perfection and receive the good tidings
that you will be rewarded; and gain strength
by worshipping in the mornings, in the nights.

— Muhammad —
(Peace be upon him)

Kindness Is Natural

Kindness is inherent in human beings.

As God is manifest in all living beings,
kindness and compassion
shown to living beings
is kindness and love shown to God.

The best form of compassion
is giving food to persons
who are unable to work
and earn their food
without questioning as
to their caste, community,
creed, color, conduct, or country. . . .

— *Jothi Ramalinga Swamigal* —

Always Be Forgiving
Always Forgive Your Brother, Sister, Neighbor, and Family

Then Peter came to Jesus
(peace be upon him) and asked,
"Lord, how many times
shall I forgive someone
when that person sins against me?
Up to seven times?"

Jesus (peace be upon him) answered,
"I tell you, not seven times,
but seventy times seven."

— The Bible —
Matthew, Chapter 18, Verses 21–22

We Are All Artists

The Sufi master Rumi
wrote about the genius within:

Inside you
there is an artist
you don't know about. . . .

Say yes quickly,
if you know,
if you have known it
from the beginning of the universe.

— Rumi —

God Is Spirit

God is spirit, and those who worship God
must worship in spirit and truth.

— Jesus —
(Peace be upon him)
The Bible, John, Chapter 4, Verse 24

Feed Hungry Children — Do Good Deeds
God Loves and Rewards the Generous Souls!

- ✳ Good deeds help make us more virtuous and please God. God rewards the virtuous!

- ✳ God's reward for virtuous behavior is Heaven.

- ✳ Feed our poor and hungry children.

- ✳ Feed our "at-risk" children and give them realistic hope for a successful and healthy life!

- ✳ We are *all* children of God.

- ✳ Give our hungry children nutritious food for their brains, bodies, and spirit to grow and develop to their God-given highest potential.

- ✳ Food is medicine that encourages hope for the hungry child.

- ✳ God loves *and* rewards those generous souls who help God's children who are in need of the basics of life!

— Robert C. Mussehl —

Maintain a Positive Perspective

When we are viewing a large painting,
we step back to gain a perspective
that includes the whole canvas
of design, color, and contrast.

We want to see and to appreciate all
that contributes to the
beauty and uniqueness of the painting.

It is important that
we have the right perspective of our lives.
If we are focusing on a challenge of life,
we may need to view the whole picture of our lives.

We can view each challenge
in its true relation and importance
to the overall picture of our lives —
lives that are filled with the goodness of God.

— Anonymous —

The Ten Righteous Commandments of God

I.   You shall have no other gods before Me.

II.   You shall not make for yourself an idol.

III.   You shall not misuse the name of the Lord, your God.

IV.   Remember the Sabbath Day by keeping it holy.

V.   Honor your father and your mother.

VI.   You shall not murder.

VII. You shall not commit adultery.

VIII. You shall not steal.

IX.   You shall not give false testimony.

X.   You shall not covet your neighbor's house, spouse, servant, or any property that belongs to your neighbor.

— The Bible —
Exodus, Chapter 20, Verses 3–17

We Are One with God

So I have turned, as you have done,
and climbed mountains and forded streams
and prayed in mosques and temples and churches
and followed teachers and stumbled and walked again
until I came to the time of evolution
when I could say truly and completely,
"I am one with God."

— Pat Rodegast & Judith Stanton —
Emmanuel's Book: A Manual For Living Comfortably in the Cosmos

A Bow Rises and Shoots

Light will someday split you open
even if your life is now a hard cage;
for a divine seed, the crown of destiny,
is hidden and sown on an ancient and fertile plain
you hold the title to.

Love will surely bust you wide open
into an unfettered, blooming new galaxy
even if your mind is now a spoiled mule.

A life-giving radiance will come —
the Friend's gratuity will come.

O look again within yourself,
for I know your soul was once the elegant host
to all the marvels in Creation.

From a sacred crevice in your body
a bow rises each night
and shoots the moon into the sky.

Behold the beautiful drunk singing one
from the lunar vantage point of love.

God is conducting the affairs
of the whole universe. ...

— *Hafiz* —

Friendship Is a Balm to the Soul

Friendship is a form of spiritual nurturance
that we are all called on to give and to receive
in everyday life; it is a balm to the soul.

The lessons of give and take learned in friendship
will elevate all of humanity to a higher standard.

If you have found a true friend,
you have come into the presence of God.

— *Hayat Abuza* —

Remember God and Be Alive!

The person who remembers God
and the other person who does not remember God
are likened to the living and the dead.

— Muhammad —
(Peace be upon him)

Choose Your Friends Carefully

People adopt a way of life
according to that of their friends,
so be careful about whom you make as a friend.

— Muhammad —
(Peace be upon him)

The Sunrise Ruby

In the early morning hour,
just before dawn,
lover and beloved
wake and take a drink of water.

She asks, "Do you love me or yourself more?
Really, tell the absolute truth."

He says, "There's nothing left of me.
I am like a ruby held up to the sunrise.
Is it still a stone, or a world made of redness?
It has no resistance to sunlight."

The ruby and the sunrise are one.
Be courageous and discipline yourself,
completely become hearing and ear,
and wear this sun-ruby as an earring.

Work. Keep digging your well.
Don't think about getting off from work.
Water is there somewhere.

Submit to a daily practice.
Your loyalty to that
is a ring on the door.

Keep knocking, and the joy inside
Will eventually open a window
And look out to see who's there.

— *Rumi* —

God Knows Everything

From God nothing is hidden on earth
or in the heavens.

— The Qur'an —
Chapter III (3), Verse 5

There Is One God

There is no God but God,
the exalted in might,
the wise.

— The Qur'an —
Chapter III (3), Verse 6

God Is Our Protector

On no soul does God place
a burden greater than it can bear.
The soul gets every good that it earns,
and it suffers every ill that it earns.

Pray to God:

Our Lord, condemn us not
if we forget or fall into error.

Our Lord, lay not on us a burden
like that which Thou (God)
did lay on those before us.

Our Lord, lay not on us a burden
greater than we have strength to bear.
Blot out our sins, and grant us forgiveness.
Have mercy on us.
You, God, are our Protector.

Help us against those who stand against faith.

— The Qur'an —
Chapter II (2), Verse 286

The Mind Is All-Powerful

Thought is a force,
even as electricity or gravitation.

The human mind is a spark of the
almighty consciousness of God.

Whatever your powerful mind
believes very intensely
would instantly come to pass.

— *Lahiri Mahasaya* —
Autobiography of a Yogi
Chapter 12

Self-Determination
You Are the *One* Who Can Make Triumphant Changes!

It doesn't matter

who you are,

or where you come from.

The ability to triumph begins with you.

Always.

— *Oprah Winfrey* —

Patience Is Essential

Patience is the foundation of wisdom.
Pray, and wait calmly and positively
for your dreams to materialize!

— Robert C. Mussehl —

Live By the Golden Rule

Do to others
as you would have them do to you.

— Jesus —
(Peace be upon him)
The Bible, Luke, Chapter 6, Verse 31

Virtue Keeps Us from the Hellfire
Virtue Takes Us to Heaven!

Jesus (peace be upon him) said:
"Devote yourself to obtaining
that which fire cannot burn."

"What is that?" asked the disciples.
"Virtue," Jesus replied.

— Dr. Javad Nurbakhsh —
Jesus in the Eyes of the Sufis

Glad Tidings of an Apostle of God
The Apostle To Come After Jesus Is Ahmad (Muhammad), Peace Be Upon Him

And remember, Jesus,
the son of Mary (peace be upon him), said:

"O Children of Israel,
I am the apostle of God sent to you
confirming the law which came before me,
and giving glad tidings
of an apostle of God to come after me.
His name shall be Ahmad
(which means 'Muhammad,'
the Praised One)."

But when Muhammad
(peace be upon him)
came to them with clear signs,
the Meccan pagans would still
not believe and said:
"This is evident sorcery!"

— The Qur'an —
Chapter LXI (61), Verse 6

Recognize God in All That You Do

Keep a fast hold on God,
and you will find God in front of you.

Recognize God in times of prosperity
and God will recognize you in times of hardship;
and know that what missed you was never to hit you,
and that what hit you was never to miss you;
and know that victory comes with patience,
and that relief comes with distress,
and that with hardship is ease.

— *Muhammad* —
(Peace be upon him)

Love Is Our Destiny

Our destiny, love, is like a stream.
When we absorb ourselves into love
we will always return to its source.

The wind will carry us home again
as the wind carries water
over the desert.

— *Anonymous* —

How To Attain Our Goals

✳ Prayer — includes faith and hope.

✳ Patience — wait calmly with optimism.

✳ Perseverance — work hard, very hard!

— Robert C. Mussehl —

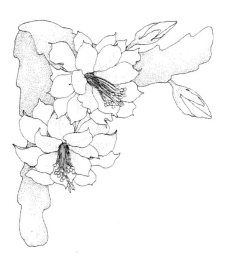

Love Is Forever

There are three things that remain:
faith, hope, and love,
and the greatest of these is love.

— The Bible —
I Corinthians, Chapter 13, Verses 4–8, 13

Love

See with the eyes of love.
Hear with the ears of love.
Work with the hands of love.
Think of love.
Feel love with every nerve.
Let love be your breath.

Let the sun of love
help the lotus of your heart to blossom.

— *Sai Baba* —

Love Each Other

Offer greetings to each other
and rancor will disappear.

Give gifts to each other and love each other,
and hatred will disappear.

— Muhammad —
(Peace be upon him)

Love First

Just love before you speak of love.

— Thakur —

Zikr (The Remembrance of God) Is a Pathway
to God's Mercy and Tranquility
God Gives a Double Reward!

✳ Whenever people sit
and remember God (Zikr),
the angels surround them,
mercy covers them,
tranquility descends upon them,
and God makes a mention of them
to His company, the angels.

✳ If you accept me as your prophet
as well as your own prophet,
God will double your rewards!

— Muhammad —
(Peace be upon him)

God's Revelation Is Our Guide
to Righteous Behavior

We believe in God,
and the revelation given to us,
and to Abraham, Isma'il, Isaac, Jacob, and the Tribes,
and that given to Moses and Jesus,
and the revelation given to all prophets
from their Lord (peace be upon them).

We make no distinction
between one and another of them,
and we submit ourselves to God.

— The Qur'an —
Chapter II (2), Verse 136

God Sends Prophets To Guide Us

Zakariya and John and Jesus and Elias
(peace be upon them)
are all in the ranks of the righteous.

And to Isma'il, Elisha, Jonas, and Lot
(peace be upon them),
God gave them favor above the nations.

To them and their fathers, progeny and brethren,
God chose them.
God guided them to a straight way.

— The Qur'an —
Chapter VI (6), Verses 85–87

The Comforter Is a Promise from God
The Comforter Will Comfort Us with Truth and Hope!
He Shall Teach Us All Things, and He, the Comforter, Will Remind
Us of the Spiritual Peace of Jesus Christ (Peace Be Upon Him)

These things I,

Jesus Christ (peace be upon him),

have spoken unto you, being yet present with you.

But, the promised comforter,

whom God shall send in my name,

he shall teach you all things,

and bring all things to your remembrance,

whatsoever I have said unto you.

Peace I leave with you,

my peace I give unto you!

Not as the world giveth,

give I unto you.

Let not your heart be troubled,

neither let it be afraid.

My peace I give unto you.

— Jesus —
(Peace be upon him)
The Bible, John, Chapter 14, Verses 25–28

My Golden Rules of Life
Develop a Passion for Compassion!

✳ Live a life of freedom.

✳ Develop a "passion for compassion" and social justice (as advocated by Rabbi Abraham Heschel and the other great, inspirational human-rights leaders throughout the centuries).

✳ Help as many people as you can along the way.

✳ Be kind, considerate, and caring.

✳ Never hurt a living soul.

✳ Follow God's law.

✳ Trust God!

✳ Never give up. Keep trying. Keep praying. Keep working hard!

— Robert C. Mussehl —

Compassion

Compassion is based on empathy,
being touched by the suffering of others.

— Judith L. Lief —

Love Is God's Greatest Gift

Love has no other desire but to fulfill itself.

But if you love and
need to have desires,
let these be your desires:

To melt and
be like a running brook
that sings its melody to the night.

To know the pain of too much tenderness.

To be wounded by
your own understanding of love.

And to bleed willingly and joyfully.

To wake at dawn
with a winged heart
and give thanks
for another day of loving.

— *Kahlil Gibran* —
The Prophet

Be Happy!

Don't worry, be happy.

— *Meher Baba* —
(popularized by musician Bobby McFerrin)

Smile Warmly

Each smile I give is a powerful message
of friendship and love.

There is no other sign in the world
that conveys friendship, love, and peace
in a more universally understood way than a smile.

A warm smile is a message of acceptance and gladness
from one person to another.

— *Anonymous* —

No Compulsion in Religion

✳ Let there be no compulsion in religion.

✳ Truth stands out clear from error.

✳ Whoever rejects evil and believes in God
has grasped the most trustworthy Handhold,
that never breaks.

✳ God hears and knows all things.

— The Qur'an —
Chapter II (2), Verse 256

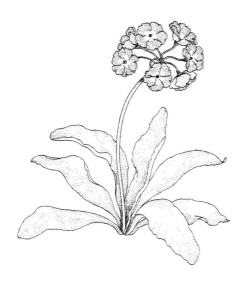

Worship God — This Is the Straight Way
The Miracles of Christ

God will teach Jesus (peace be upon him)
the book, the wisdom, the law, and the gospel.
God will appoint Jesus, the Christ (peace be upon him),
an apostle to the children of Israel
with this message:

"I have come to you with signs from God in that —

✶ I make for you, out of clay, the figure
of a bird, and breathe into it, and
it becomes a bird, by God's leave.

✶ I heal those born blind.

✶ I heal the lepers.

✶ I quicken the dead, by God's leave.

Surely these miracles are signs for you
if you did believe.

Then worship God.
This is a way that is straight."

— The Qur'an —
Chapter III (3), Verses 48, 49, 51

Core Daily Affirmations

- ✳ God is Perfect.

- ✳ God's plan is Perfect.

- ✳ God's plan for me is Perfect.

- ✳ I surrender to God.

- ✳ God is Love!

— Robert C. Mussehl —

Love Sustains, Love Remains
Love Is Our Purpose!

Life has pressure and pain.
We need love to sustain.

With love we feel vital and alive.
Love strengthens our will to survive.

We need love to overcome our pain.
Love is our purpose. Love always remains.

Love has always been our purpose.
Love will *always* be our purpose!

— Robert C. Mussehl —

The Miracles of Birth and Heaven Are Easy for God

Rumi (1207 to 1273),
the Sufi poet and mystic of Persia,
described the virgin birth of Jesus
(peace be upon him)
in a lovely, mystical poem.

The Sufis believe that
Jesus was born of Mary
through the breath
of the Holy Spirit
and had no physical father.

— *Dr. Javad Nurbakhsh* —
Jesus in the Eyes of the Sufis

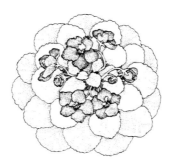

Affirmations of Peace

⚹   Today and at all times, I will be peaceful,
calm, friendly, patient, positive, supportive,
tolerant, forgiving, happy, and fully satisfied.

⚹   I am always grateful to God.

⚹   I have no fear or anger because
I trust God completely.

— Robert C. Mussehl —

God Has Enormous Love for Me

⚹   God *loves* me!

⚹   God loves me *more* than the combined love
of seventy of the most loving, kind, generous,
protective, nurturing, and sweetest mothers
who ever lived in this world.

⚹   God's will for me is perfect happiness.

— Robert C. Mussehl —

How To Get to Heaven
A Message from God to the Righteous Believers!

If you guarantee God six things on your part,
God shall guarantee you Paradise:

I.   Speak the truth when you talk.

II. Keep a promise when you make it.

III. When you are trusted with something,
     fulfill your trust.

IV. Avoid sexual immorality.

V.   Lower your gaze out of modesty.

VI. Restrain your hands from injustice.

— *Muhammad* —
(Peace be upon him)

Remember and Praise God

✳ There is nothing to worship but God —
    the one without a partner.

✳ God is the dominion.

✳ All praise belongs to God.

✳ God has power over everything.

— Muhammad —
(Peace be upon him)

Do Not Miss an Opportunity

There are many opportunities to work
with the experience of change,
since every single day
is filled with transitions
that for the most part go unnoticed.

— *Judith L. Lief* —

Friendship

If you maintain a feeling of compassion
and loving kindness, then something
automatically opens your inner door.

Through that, you can communicate
more easily with other people.
And that feeling of warmth
creates a kind of openness.

You'll find that all human beings
are just like you,
so you'll be able to relate to them more easily.

That gives you a spirit of friendship.

— The Dalai Lama —
The Art of Happiness

Walk in the Shoes of Others

I think empathy is important,
not only as a means of enhancing compassion,
but I think that generally speaking,
when dealing with others on any level,
if you are having some difficulties,
it is extremely helpful to be able
to put yourself in the other person's place
and see how you would react to the situation.

— The Dalai Lama —

Be Confident in All That You Do

A healthy sense of self-confidence
is a critical factor
in achieving our goals.

— The Dalai Lama —

The Glory of God Is Within Our Hearts
Let Our Own Light Shine Brightly!

Our deepest fear is not that we are inadequate.

Our deepest fear is that we are powerful beyond measure.

It is our light, not our darkness, that most frightens us.

We ask ourselves,

who am I to be brilliant, gorgeous, talented, and fabulous?

Actually, who are you not to be?

You are a child of God.

Your playing small does not serve the world.

There is nothing enlightened about shrinking

so that other people won't feel insecure around you.

We are born to manifest the glory of God that is within us.

It is not just in some of us; it is in everyone.

And as we let our own light shine,

we unconsciously give other people

permission to do the same.

As we are liberated from our own fear,

our presence automatically liberates others.

— *Marianne Williamson* —
A Return to Love

Persevere

You, who believe,
seek help with
patient perseverance and prayer.

God is with those
who patiently persevere.

— The Qur'an —
Chapter II (2), Verse 153

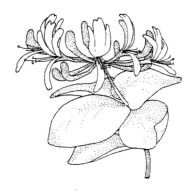

Believe in God

To those who believe in
God and God's apostles
and make no distinction
between any of the apostles,
we shall soon give them
their due rewards.

God is the most forgiving,
the most merciful.

— The Qur'an —
Chapter IV (4), Verse 152

Make Life Count

Life will pass by in a blink of the eye.
Unknown lands and species are yet to be discovered.

Blue waters and mystic lagoons are awaiting;
people of all tribes and nations
need a new face and soul to listen.

Material gain is not ours for the keeping.
We will not take along these possessions when we die.

Only our memories are engraved in our hearts,
and our behavior and good deeds will count.

— *Anonymous* —

PARADISE

Heaven Is Our Destination

At last you've left and gone to the Invisible;
how marvelous the way you quit this world.

You ruffled your feathers and,
breaking free of your cage,
you took to the air,
bound for your soul's world. ...

A love-sick nightingale among owls,
you caught the scent of roses,
and flew to the rose garden.

— *Rumi* —

We Never Die

Death is like taking off a tight shoe.

Even when you are dead, you are still alive.
You do not cease to exist at death.
That is only an illusion.

You go through the doorway of death alive
and there is no altering of the consciousness.

It is not a strange land you go to
but a land of living reality
where the growth process is a continuation.

— *Pat Rodegast & Judith Stanton* —
Emmanuel's Book: A Manual For Living Comfortably in the Cosmos

Love and Forgiveness Is the Path Toward Heaven
Jesus Is a Role Model for Our Roadway to Heaven

Muhammad (peace be upon him)
confirmed that the mission of Jesus
(peace be upon him) and his message
of loving and forgiving each other
was real and authentic.

Muhammad (peace be upon him) stated further
that we will not enter Heaven
unless we believe in God
and that we love and forgive one another,
as prescribed and commanded by Jesus
(peace be upon him).

— *Robert C. Mussehl* —
(also the Bible, John, Chapter 13, Verses 34–35)

Heaven Is Safe and Secure

Jesus (peace be upon him)
said to his disciples:

"Do not store up for yourselves treasures on earth,
where moth and rust must destroy,
and where thieves break in and steal.

But, store up for yourselves treasures in Heaven,
where moth and rust do not destroy,
and where thieves do not break in and steal.

For where your treasure is,
there your heart will be also."

— The Bible —
Matthew, Chapter 6, Verses 19–21

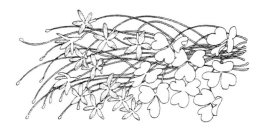

We Are Immortal Beings
We Do Not Die!

I have now told you,
Yogananda, the truths of my
life, death, and resurrection!

Grieve not for me!
Rather broadcast everywhere
the story of my resurrection!

— Swami Sri Yukteswar —
Autobiography of a Yogi
Chapter 43

God Is Our Destiny

We are travelers —
We live on a spaceship and in a space suit
And God is our home port!

— Robert C. Mussehl —

Love God!
God Has Prepared the Finest for Those Who Love God

No eye has seen,

no ear has heard,

no mind has conceived

what God has prepared

for those who love God!

— The Bible —
1 Corinthians, Chapter 2, Verse 9

We Can Make It to Paradise
God Created Us to Live with God
and with God's Righteous Servants *Forever* in Heaven!

All things are possible to them that believe!

— Jesus —
(Peace be upon him)
The Bible, Mark, Chapter 9, Verse 23

Reminders of God's Mercy and Sovereignty
God Rules the Universe. God Rules Heaven!

* ❋   God is our Protector!

* ❋   God is peace.

* ❋   God is love.

* ❋   God is merciful.

* ❋   God is forgiving.

* ❋   God rules the heavens and the universe.

* ❋   God rewards the righteous with Paradise!

— Robert C. Mussehl —

Our Heavenly Home

God's house has many mansions!

— Jesus —
(Peace be upon him)
The Bible, John, Chapter 14, Verses 2

Jesus (Peace Be Upon Him)
Is Proof of Our Immortality

Indubitably no person is born fatherless.
Only one, Jesus (peace be upon him),
exists in the world.

— Sheikh Mahmud Shabistari —
Jesus in the Eyes of the Sufis

Love Rules the Court
Love Is Heaven! Heaven Is Love!

Love rules the court,

the camp, the grove,

the men and women below

and saints above;

for love is Heaven

and Heaven is love.

— Sir Walter Scott —
The Lay of the Last Minstrel

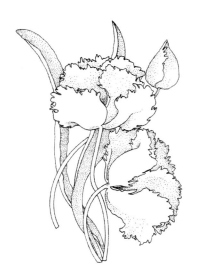

God Rules His Kingdom Forever

Then the seventh angel sounded,
and there were loud voices
in Heaven, saying:

"The kingdoms of this world
have become the kingdoms
of our Lord and of His Christ,
and He shall reign forever and ever."

— The Bible —
Revelation, Chapter 11, Verse 15

God Will Create a Kingdom
Which Shall Never Be Destroyed

And in the days of these kings,

the God of Heaven

will set up a kingdom

which shall never be destroyed;

and the kingdom shall not

be left to other people;

it shall break in pieces

and consume all these kingdoms,

and it shall stand forever.

— The Bible —
Daniel, Chapter 2, Verse 44

God Enthrones the Righteous

God does not take his eyes off the righteous.
God enthrones them with kings and exalts them forever.

— The Bible —
Job, Chapter 36, Verse 7

We Were Created To Be Immortal

The resurrected Yukteswar revealed to Yogananda:
"God encased the immortal human soul
successively in three bodies:

* ✳ The idea — or causal body (the heavenly body).

* ✳ The subtle astral body — the seat of a person's
mental and emotional natures.

* ✳ The gross physical body."

— Swami Sri Yukteswar —
Autobiography of a Yogi
Chapter 43

God Rewards Patience and Good Deeds

God will render to each one
according to his or her deeds:
eternal life to those
who by patient continuance in doing good
seek for glory, honor, and immortality.

— The Bible —
Romans, Chapter 2, Verses 6–7

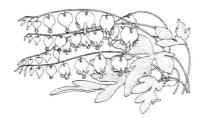

God Promises Us Eternal Life

We have the hope of eternal life
that God, who cannot lie,
promised before time began.

— The Bible —
Titus, Chapter 1, Verse 2

Heaven Is Made for Us

Now we know that if the earthly tent
we live in is destroyed,
we have a building from God,
an external house in Heaven
not built by human hands. . . .

Now it is God who has made us
for this very purpose
and has given us
the spirit as a deposit,
guaranteeing what is to come.

— The Bible —
II Corinthians, Chapter 5, Verses 1, 5

God Leads the Way to Heaven

God will admit those who believe
and work righteous deeds to the gardens
beneath which rivers flow.

They shall be adorned
with bracelets of gold and pearls;
and their garments will be
of fine and luxurious silk.

For they have been guided in this life
to the purest of speeches;
they have been guided to the path of God.

— The Qur'an —
Chapter XXII (22), Verses 23–24

Drink the Water of Bliss

Truly the righteous will be in bliss;
on thrones of dignity they will command
a majestic sight of all things!

You will recognize in their faces
the beaming brightness of bliss;
their thirst will be satisfied
with pure wine sealed.

The seal thereof will be of musk;
drink with delight!

Those who have aspirations
will attain their aspirations with certainty!

With it will be given a mixture of tasnīm:
a spring from the waters
that those nearest to God drink!

— The Qur'an —
Chapter LXXXIII (83), Verses 22–28

Heaven Provides Peace and Security

My devotees!
You shall have no fear on that day nor shall you grieve.

Being those who have believed in God's signs
and bowed their wills to God.
Enter you into the Garden,
you and your spouses in beauty and rejoicing!

To them will be passed around dishes
and goblets of gold —
there will be in Heaven all that a soul could desire!

All that the eyes could delight in;
And there you shall dwell forever!
Such will be the Garden of which
you are made heirs, for your good deeds in life.

You shall have in the Garden, abundance of fruit,
from which you shall have satisfaction.

— The Qur'an —
Chapter XLIII (43), Verses 68–73

God Provides Perfect Justice
The Righteous Shall Enter Paradise!

And those who feared their Lord will be led
in crowds to the Garden until behold, they arrive there;
and its gates will be opened; and its keepers will say:
"Peace be upon you! Well have you done!
Enter Paradise to dwell inside."

They will say: "Praise be to God,
who has truly fulfilled His promise to us,
and has given us this land in heritage;
we can dwell in the Garden as we will;
how excellent a reward for those
who work in righteousness!"

And you will see the angels surrounding
the throne divine on all sides,
singing glory and praise to their Lord.

The decision between them at judgment
will be in perfect justice, and the cry on all sides will be:
"Praise be to God, the Lord of the Worlds!'

— The Qur'an —
Chapter XXXIX (39), Verses 73–75

The Righteous Will Be Rewarded

Blessed is God who, if that were God's will,
could give you better things than those,
gardens beneath which rivers flow,
and God could give you palaces secure to dwell in.

The eternal Garden is a promise to the righteous …
for them is a reward
as well as the goal of attainment.

For them there will be in that place
all they wish for;
they will dwell in Heaven forever.

A promise to be prayed for from the Lord.

— The Qur'an —
Chapter XXV (25), Verses 10, 15, 16

Our Greatest Reward Is the Presence of God

Those who believe, and suffer exile,

and strive with might in God's cause,

with their goods and their persons,

have the highest rank in the sight of God;

they are the people who will attain salvation.

Their Lord does give them glad tidings of mercy

from Himself, of God's good pleasure,

and of gardens for them, in which delights endure.

They will dwell in Heaven forever;

in God's presence is a reward, the greatest of all.

— The Qur'an —
Chapter IX (9), Verses 20–22

You Will *Always* Have Energy in Heaven! ☼
God Removes Any Lurking Sense of Injury!

The righteous will be amid gardens
and fountains of clear-flowing water.

Their greeting will be,
"Enter Heaven in peace and security."

And We shall remove from their hearts
any lurking sense of injury;
they will be brothers and sisters
joyfully facing each other on thrones of dignity.

In Heaven, no feeling of fatigue shall touch them!
Nor shall they ever be asked to leave.

Tell My servants that I am indeed
the most merciful, the most forgiving.

— The Qur'an —
Chapter (XV) 15, Verses 45–49

God Rewards Those Who Follow God's Law

And the Garden will be brought close
to the righteous,
no more a thing distant.

A voice will say:
"This is what was promised to you,
for everyone who turned to God
in sincere repentance,
who kept God's law.

Who feared God most gracious unseen,
and brought a heart
turned in devotion to God.

Enter in peace and security!
This is a day of eternal life!

There will be for them
all that they wish,
and more besides, in Our presence!"

— *The Qur'an* —
Chapter L (50), Verses 31–35

Each Good Deed Counts
The Righteous Will Be in Gardens of Eternity!

As to those who believe and work in righteousness,
We shall not waste the reward of any person
who does a single righteous deed.

For them will be Gardens of Eternity,
beneath them rivers will flow.
They will be adorned with bracelets of gold,
and they will wear green garments
of fine silk and heavy brocade;
they will recline on raised thrones.
How good the payment!
How beautiful a couch to recline on!

— The Qur'an —
Chapter XVIII (18), Verses 30–31

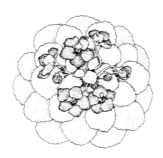

God Can Easily Create Paradise
Mary Is Our Virtuous Role Model

Behold!

The angel Gabriel said: "O Mary!

God has chosen you and purified you.

God has chosen you above the women of all nations."

Mary said: "O my Lord!

How shall I have a son when no man has touched me?"

Gabriel said: "Even so, God creates what God wills.

When God has decreed a plan,

God says to it, 'Be,' and it is!"

— The Qur'an —
Chapter III (3), Verses 42, 47

God Is the Supreme Power
Serve God! God the Most Gracious Has Promised
Gardens of Eternity to God's Servants

Those who repent with sincerity and honesty
in their conduct and believe,
and work righteousness will enter the Garden
and will not be wronged in the least.

Gardens of eternity are those
which God most gracious has promised to His servants,
for God's promise must necessarily come to pass!

In Heaven they will not hear vain discourse;
they will hear only salutations of peace;
they will have their sustenance,
morning and evening in Heaven.

Such is the Garden which we give as an inheritance
to our servants who guard against evil.

The angels say:
"We descend by command of our Lord;
to God belongs what is before us,

and what is behind us and what is between;
and our Lord never does forget.

The Lord of the heavens, and of the earth,
and of all that is between them!

Worship God
and be constant and patient in your worship of God.

Do you know of any who is worthy
of the same name as God?
(God the Almighty)

The one and only God
of the universe, the Supreme Power!"

— *The Qur'an* —
Chapter XIX (19), Verses 60–65

Fasting Is Like a Shield
God Reserves a Private Door to Paradise
for Those Who Fast To Please God

Fasting is like a shield,
and persons who fast have two joys:
joy when they break their fast,
and joy when they meet their Lord.

— *Muhammad* —
(Peace be upon him)

Help the Poor
Be Near God on the Day of Resurrection!

If you love the poor and bring them near you,
God will bring you near Him
on the day of Resurrection.

— *Muhammad* —
(Peace be upon him)

From Suffering Comes Spiritual Rewards
Our Promised Home Is Heaven!

Every heartache and suffering
that enters your body and heart
pulls you to the promised home.

— *Rumi* —

Praise God
All Goodness Flows from God's Eternal Fountain of Love

God is infinite mercy. God is perfect peace.

God is the most forbearing. God is the greatest.

God is the most trustworthy.

God is the remover of all afflictions.

God is the self-sufficient.

God is supreme. God is our King.

God is the light of Heaven and earth.

God is worthy of all praise. God is the most forgiving.

God is the provider!

God is exalted in power. God is our safeguard.

God is the fountain of all goodness!

— *Robert C. Mussehl* —

The Believers Hear and Obey God
God Is the End of Our Journey!

The apostle believes in
what has been revealed
to him from his Lord, as do men and women of faith.

Each one of them believes in God's angels,
God's books, and God's apostles.

God makes no distinction
between one and another of God's apostles.

And they say: "We hear and we obey.
We seek Your forgiveness, our Lord,
and to You, God, is the end of all journeys."

— The Qur'an —
Chapter II (2), Verse 285

God Rewards Goodness —
All Righteous Believers Are Headed for Heaven!

Christians, Jews, and Muslims
Shall Have Their Reward with God in Heaven!

✳   Those who believe in the Qur'an,
     and those who follow the Jewish scripture
     and the Christian scripture....

✳   Those who believe in God and the Last Day,
     and work righteousness,
     shall have their reward with their Lord.

✳   On them shall be no fear,
     nor shall they grieve.

— The Qur'an —
Chapter II (2), Verse 62

The Road to Heaven Is Charity
Charity Is Our *Collective* Responsibility

Each person must perform
a charity every day the sun comes up:

※ To act justly between two persons
is a charity.

※ To help persons with their mount,
lifting them onto it, or hoisting up
their belongings onto it, is a charity.

※ A good word is charity.

※ Every step you take to prayers is a charity.

※ Removing a harmful thing from the road
is a charity.

— Muhammad —
(Peace be upon him)

There Is No Toil or Weariness in Heaven

We have given the holy books
to our pure and faithful servants (God's prophets)
as Our trustees to convey Our sacred message.

Some people wrong their own souls;
some souls follow a middle course;
and some souls are, by God's leave,
foremost in good deeds; that is the highest grace.

The gardens of eternity will they enter,
where they will be adorned with bracelets of gold and pearls;
and their garments will be of silk.

And they will say: "Praise be to God,
Who has removed from us all sorrow;
for our Lord is indeed oft-forgiving,
ready to appreciate service.

Who has, out of God's bounty, settled us
in a heavenly home that will last;
no toil or weariness shall touch us therein."

— *The Qur'an* —
Chapter XXXV (35), Verses 32–35

There Are Fruits and Delights in Heaven

For sincere and devoted servants of God,
there will be sustenance, fruits, and delights;
and they shall enjoy honor and dignity!

In the Gardens of Felicity,
facing each other on thrones of dignity,
passed around to them will be a cup
from a clear-flowing fountain, crystal-clear,
of a taste delicious to those
who drink thereof, free from headiness.

Nor will they suffer intoxication thereof,
and beside them will be chaste companions
restraining their glances,
with big eyes of wonder and beauty.

As if they were
delicate eggs closely guarded.

— The Qur'an —
Chapter XXXVII (37), Verses 40–49

God's Promise of Paradise Will Never Fail
Heaven Is a Beautiful Place of Final Return

This is a message of admonition:
For the righteous person,
Heaven is a beautiful place of final return.

Gardens of Eternity,
whose doors will be open forever to the righteous,
therein can they call, at leisure,
for pleasure of fruit in abundance,
and for delicious drink.

And beside them will be chaste companions
restraining their glances.

Such is the promise made to you for the day of account!

Truly such will be Our bounty to you;
it will never fail.

— The Qur'an —
Chapter XXXVIII (38), Verses 49–54

Heavenly Mansions Are Ours To Claim

It is for those
who fear their Lord
that lofty mansions,
one above the other,
have been built.

Beneath them flow
rivers of delight!

The promise of God
is always kept!

— The Qur'an —
Chapter XXXIX (39), Verse 20

God Always Forgives Us
The Righteous Shall Be Given All They Wish!

Those who believe and work righteous deeds
will be in the luxuriant meads of the gardens;
they shall be given all that they wish!
That will indeed be the magnificent bounty of God.

That is the bounty which God gives glad tidings
to God's servants who believe and do righteous deeds.

God says to Muhammad (peace be upon him),
"Tell the people that I, Muhammad, do not ask
for any reward from you except the love of kin."

If anyone earns any good,
We shall give that person an increase of good.
God is oft-forgiving, and ready to appreciate service!

— The Qur'an —
Chapter XLII (42), Verses 22–23

Being Charitable Brings Great Rewards

Believe in God Almighty
and God's apostles
and spend in charity
out of what
God made you trustees of.

For those of you who believe in God
and spend in charity for them
are great rewards.

— The Qur'an —
Chapter LVII (57), Verse 7

In the Garden Are Pure Rivers

There is a parable of the Garden
in which the righteous are promised
rivers of water incorruptible, and
never-changing rivers of milk
that are always delicious to taste!

And rivers of wine,
joyful to those who drink;
rivers pure and clear.
In the Garden are all kinds of fruits,
and grace from their Lord.

— The Qur'an —
Chapter XLVII (47), Verse 15

Good Deeds Are Rewarded

For those who believe and do righteous deeds
are gardens as hospitable homes,
rewards for their good deeds.

— The Qur'an —
Chapter XXXII (32), Verse 19

The Righteous Will Be in Gardens

As to the righteous,
they will be in the midst of gardens and rivers,
assembled in the presence of truth,
the sovereign, omnipotent.

— The Qur'an —
Chapter LIV (54), Verses 54–55

Obeying God Is the Straight Way to Paradise
(The Second Coming of Christ)

And Jesus, the Christ
(peace be upon him), shall be a sign —
an unmistakable sign of the hour of judgment!

Therefore, have no doubt about the hour
of judgment, but follow God, obey God.
This is the straight way.

— The Qur'an —
Chapter XLIII (43), Verses 61–64

Heaven Is Bliss!
You Can Eat and Drink in Heaven with Full Satisfaction

You will be in a life of bliss,
in a garden on high.
The fruits in Heaven will hang
in bunches low and near.

Eat and drink with full satisfaction
because of the good deeds on earth
that you sent to Us from the days that are gone!

— The Qur'an —
Chapter LXIX (69), Verses 21–24

God's Bounty Is Eternal!

As to the righteous,
they shall drink of a cup of wine
mixed with Kafur —
a fountain that flows forever!

The more devotees of God
drink from the fountain,
the more the fountain
flows in abundance.

— The Qur'an —
Chapter LXXVI (76), Verses 5–6

In Heaven We Will Be More Than Satisfied!

Faces on that day will be joyful,
pleased with their striving
in a garden on high,
where they shall hear no word of vanity;
therein will be a bubbling spring;
therein will be thrones of dignity raised on high.

Goblets of gold and precious jewels
and crystals are placed ready,
and beautiful and comfortable cushions set in rows,
and rich carpets all spread out.

— The Qur'an —
Chapter LXXXVIII (88), Verses 8–16

God's Gardens Are Reserved for Those with Excellent Moral Conduct!

For such human beings who fear the time when
they will stand before the judgment seat of their Lord,
and do daily good deeds and have excellent moral conduct,
there will be two gardens.
Then which of the favors of your Lord will you deny?

Containing all kinds of trees and delights,
then which of the favors of your Lord will you deny?
In each garden will be two springs flowing free;
then which of the favors of your Lord will you deny?
In them will be fruits of every kind, two and two;
then which of the favors of your Lord will you deny?

The righteous will recline on carpets,
whose inner linings will be of rich brocade;
the fruit of the gardens will be near and easy to reach.
Then which of the favors of your Lord will you deny?

In the gardens will be chaste companions restraining
their glances, whom no person before them has touched;
then which of the favors of your Lord will you deny?
Like unto rubies and coral,
then which of the favors of your Lord will you deny?
Is there any reward for good other than good?
Then which of the favors of your Lord will you deny?

And besides these two, there are two other gardens;
then which of the favors of your Lord will you deny?
Dark green in color from plentiful watering,
then which of the favors of your Lord will you deny?

In them will be two springs pouring forth
delicious-tasting water in continuous abundance;
then which of the favors of your Lord will you deny?
In them will be fruits and dates and pomegranates;
then which of the favors of your Lord will you deny?
In them will be fair companions, good, beautiful;
then which of the favors of your Lord will you deny?

Companions restrained as to their glances,
in goodly pavilions;
then which of the favors of your Lord will you deny?
Whom no person before them has touched;
then which of the favors of your Lord will you deny?

Reclining on beautiful and comfortable cushions
and rich carpets of elegant design and with rainbows of color;
then which of the favors of your Lord will you deny?

Blessed be the name of our Lord, full of majesty,
bounty and honor.

— The Qur'an —
Chapter LV (55), Verses 46–78

The Best Souls Are the Righteous

Those who have faith and do righteous deeds,
they are the best of creatures.

Their reward is with God:
Gardens of eternity, beneath which rivers flow;
they will dwell therein, forever,
God well pleased with them
and they with God.

All this for those souls
that fear the displeasure
of their Lord and cherisher,
and act in righteousness.

— The Qur'an —
Chapter XCVIII (98), Verses 7–8

Give and God Will Give to You
God Promises Us Beautiful Mansions and Gardens of Everlasting Bliss!

The believers, men and women,
are protectors, one of another.
They encourage what is just, and forbid what is evil;
they observe regular prayers,
practice regular charity,
and obey God and the laws
that God has given His apostles.

On the believers, God will pour His mercy:
For God is exalted in power, wise.

God has promised to believers, men and women,
gardens for them to dwell within,
under which rivers flow, and beautiful mansions
in the gardens of everlasting bliss,
but the greatest bliss
is the good pleasure of God.

That is the supreme felicity,
the supreme joy and happiness!

— *The Qur'an* —
Chapter IX (9), Verses 71–72

The Truthful Will Be Rewarded

In Heaven, *All* of Our Desires Are *Fully* Satisfied!

God will say:
"This is a day in which the truthful
will profit from their truth;
there are gardens with rivers
flowing beneath their eternal home.

God is well-pleased with them, and they with God;
that is the great salvation,
the fulfillment of all desires.

To God belongs the dominion
of the heavens and the earth, and all that is therein,
and it is God who has power over all things."

— The Qur'an —
Chapter V (5), Verses 122–123

God Brings Us Peace
We Will Be in Cool, Shaded Groves
Reclining on Thrones of Dignity

The companions of the Garden shall
on that day have joy in what they do.

They will be in cool shaded groves,
reclining on thrones of dignity.

Every fruit and enjoyment will be there for them;
they shall have whatever they call for.

"Peace!"
A word of salutation from God most merciful!

— The Qur'an —
Chapter XXXVI (36), Verses 55–58

Every Good Deed Counts
We Shall Have Pure and Holy Companions!

Those who believe and do deeds of righteousness,
We shall soon admit to Gardens
with rivers flowing beneath, their eternal home,
where they shall have companions pure and holy;
We shall admit them to shades, cool and ever deepening.

— The Qur'an —
Chapter IV (4), Verse 57

God's Invitation to the Righteous!

To the righteous soul will be said:
"Rest in complete satisfaction!
You have come back to your Lord!
Well-pleased with God and well-pleasing unto God!
Enter Heaven and dwell among My devotees.
Enter My precious Heaven!"

— The Qur'an —
Chapter LXXXIX (89), Verses 27–30

God Knows the Unseen

God is the knower of the unseen.

Not an atom's weight escapes God
in the heavens or in the earth.
It is all recorded in a clear record.

God Almighty will reward
those who believe
and do good works.

For them is pardon, forgiveness,
and a rich provision!

— The Qur'an —
Chapter XXXIV (34), Verses 3–4

God Gives Us Justice Forever

If anyone does
deeds of righteousness,
whether male or female, and either has faith,
she and he will enter Heaven,
and not the least injustice
will be done to them.

Who can be better in religion
than those who submit
their whole selves to God,
do good, and follow the way
of Abraham — the true and sincere — in faith?
(Peace be upon him.)
For God did take Abraham (peace be upon him)
for a friend.

All things in the heavens
and earth belong to God;
God encompasses all things.
God is the dominion.

— The Qur'an —
Chapter IV (4), Verses 124–126

God Honors the Trustworthy
The Trustworthy Will Be the Honored Ones in the Garden of Bliss!

And those who respect

their trusts and covenants,

and those who stand firm

in their testimonies,

and those who guard the sacredness

of their worship:

Such will be the honored ones

in the Garden of Bliss.

— The Qur'an —
Chapter LXX (70), Verses 32–35

Self-Discipline Is Rewarded!
God Honors Those Who Control Their Lower Desires
With a Residence in the Eternal Garden of Paradise!

And for such persons

who considered the fear of standing

before their Lord's tribunal

and had restrained their souls

from lower desires,

their dwelling will be in the eternal Garden!

— The Qur'an —
Chapter LXXIX (79), Verses 40–41

God's Perfect World Includes Heaven for Us

It is God that created for you
all things that are on earth.

Moreover, God's design
comprehended the heavens,
for God gave order and perfection
to the seven firmaments.
God has perfect knowledge of all things.

— The Qur'an —
Chapter II (2), Verse 29

Heaven Is Happiness Supreme

As to the righteous,
they will be in Gardens,
and in happiness,
enjoying the bliss
which God has bestowed on them,
and God shall deliver them
from the penalty of the fire.

To them will be said:
"Eat and drink all that you like
with profit and health,
because of your good deeds.

They will recline with ease
on thrones of dignity
arranged in ranks;
and We shall unite them with companions
whose eyes are big, beautiful, and lustrous.

And those believers whose families
follow them in faith,
to them shall We join their families.

Nor shall We deprive them
of the fruit of their works;
each individual is responsible
for his or her deeds.

And We shall bestow on them
fruit, nuts, and meat,
anything they shall desire.

In Heaven they shall exchange
with each other a loving cup free of frivolity,
free of all taint of ill.

Around about them
will serve, devoted to them,
youths handsome as pearls well-guarded."

— The Qur'an —
Chapter LII (52), Verses 17–24

God's Word Is Most True

Those who believe and
do deeds of righteousness,
God shall soon admit them to gardens,
with rivers flowing beneath
to dwell therein forever.

God's promise is the truth,
and whose word can be truer
than God's word?

— The Qur'an —
Chapter IV (4), Verse 122

God Gives Us Glad Tidings
Heaven Is Forever!

Give glad tidings to those
who believe and work righteousness,
that their portion is gardens
beneath which rivers flow.

Every time they are fed
with fruits therefrom, they say,
"Why, this is what
we were fed with before."

For they are given things in similitude.
They shall have in Heaven
companions pure and holy.
They will abide in Heaven forever.

— The Qur'an —
Chapter II (2), Verse 25

To God Shall We Return

How can you reject the faith in God?

Seeing that you were without life,
God gave you life.

Then God will cause you to die
and God will again bring you to life.

Again to God shall you return.

— The Qur'an —
Chapter II (2), Verse 28

The Believers Will Prosper!
The Believers Will Be in Heaven!

This is the book (the Qur'an).
In it is guidance sure, without doubt,
to those who fear God.

And to those souls who believe in the unseen, and who —

* are steadfast in prayer,

* spend out of what God has provided for them,

* believe in the Revelations sent to thee, Muhammad
  (peace be upon him),

* and the Revelations sent to God's prophets
  before your time,

* and — in their hearts — have the assurance
  of the Hereafter (Heaven).

They are on true guidance from their Lord,
and it is these who will prosper.

— The Qur'an —
Chapter II (2), Verses 2–5

The Good Are Rewarded!
Heaven Is Our Final Destination!

God gave Abraham a son,
Isaac, and grandson, Jacob.

God guided all three (peace be upon them).

Before Abraham, God guided Noah and his progeny,
David, Solomon, Job, Joseph, Moses, and Aaron
(peace and blessings be upon
all of God's prophets).

God rewards those who do good.

— The Qur'an —
Chapter VI (6), Verse 84

Our Lord Is Most Bountiful

Read or proclaim
in the name of our Lord,
who created men and women
from a clot of congealed blood.

Read or proclaim that
our Lord is most bountiful.

God taught us
the use of the pen,
and God taught men and women
that which they knew not.

— The Qur'an —
Chapter XCVI (96), Verses 1–5

Heaven Is the Best Place

The minutest place in the Garden
is better than this world
and everything in it.

— Muhammad —
(Peace be upon him)

Life Is Eternal

Our death is our wedding with eternity.

What is the secret?

God is ONE. . . .

— Rumi —

SOURCES

HAYAT NANCY ABUZA (UNKNOWN)

Hayat Nancy Abuza is an ordained interfaith chaplain and the interfaith program coordinator at Smith College in Massachusetts, where she leads the Wellness Initiative. Abuza received her B.A. from Harvard and her M.D. from Albany Medical College in 1981. She teaches meditation, stress reduction, guided visualization, and sacred arts at Smith and Amherst Colleges. A haiku poet, she also leads classes, workshops, and retreats, drawing from her background in complementary medicine, psychology, and yoga.

AMMACHI (SRI MATA AMRITANANDAMAYI DEVI) (1953 –)

Mata Amritanandamayi was born in a small coastal village in India, where her parents noticed that she bore signs of spirituality from her birth. Ammachi or Amma, as she is known, has devoted her life to helping innumerable humanitarian services and creating institutions, including the Amrita University and School of Medicine in India. She has earned international recognition by the United Nations for her outstanding contributions to the world community and as a spiritual leader. Amma says: "Compassion to the poor and needy is our duty to God." Through the example of her own life, Amma has inspired people from all over the world to walk in the path of selfless compassion and service toward all beings.

ST. TERESA OF AVILA (1515 – 1582)

Born in Spain, St. Teresa began life as the daughter of a merchant, one of ten children. After her mother's death, she was entrusted to the care of Augustinian nuns. Teresa's unusually passionate religious devotion compelled her in turn to become a nun. During her early years in the convent, she suffered from a severe illness that left her legs paralyzed for three years, but her subsequent, healing vision of "the sorely wounded Christ" profoundly changed her life. She worked as a reformer, founded numerous convents in Spain, and is known for her unusually poignant mystical writings, which include *The Interior Castle,* her autobiography, and *The Way of Perfection.* St. Teresa died in 1582 and was canonized in 1622.

MERWAN SHERIAR IRANI (MEHER BABA) (1894 – 1969)

Unlike many of his contemporaries, Merwan showed no spiritual inclination until late adolescence, when he met and studied with five gurus, including Sai Baba. Eventually he began attracting followers of his own and was given the name "Meher Baba," or "Compassionate Father." In particular, he was noted for his verbal silence, which he maintained from 1925 to his death in 1969, and he communicated through the use of an alphabet board and hand gestures. The expression, "Don't worry, be happy," which was made famous by Bobby McFerrin's number-one U.S. hit song of the same name in 1988, is what Baba frequently used in cabling messages to his followers in the West.

Sathya Sai Baba (1926 –)

Sathya Sai Baba was born in Puttaparthi, India, where as a child, he demonstrated tremendous compassion, generosity, and wisdom. At the age of fourteen, he declared to his family and to the people that he would be known as Sai Baba, and that his mission was to start a spiritual regeneration of humanity by demonstrating and teaching the highest principles of truth, righteous conduct, peace, and divine love. He has founded several Indian institutions and services projects, such as the Sri Sathya Institution of Higher Medical Science, Sri Sathya General Hospital, and clean water projects.

The Bible

In its most widely recognized form, the Bible is considered by Christians to be the inspired record of God's revelation of Himself and of His will to humankind. Written over a period of 3,500 years, "The Book," as it is sometimes called, is a collection of ancient writings that includes the books of both the Old Testament and the New Testament, which are used by the Christian Church. The Bible can also refer to the Hebrew Scriptures (the sacred book of Judaism) or, more generically, to a book or collection of writings constituting the sacred text of any religion.

The Bible, as used by most Christians, includes the Hebrew Scripture (including the books of Daniel and Job) and the New Testament, which relates the life and teachings of Jesus (peace be upon him), the letters of the Apostle Paul and other disciples to the early Church, and the Book of Revelation. The Hebrew Bible contains common portions of both Christian and Jewish biblical canons, including the Old Testament, which covers Genesis and God's creation of the world and His early relationship with humanity.

Mahatma Gandhi (1869 – 1948)

Mahatma Gandhi is one of the seminal figures of the twentieth century, recognized for his political and spiritual leadership through asceticism and the practice of nonviolence. Gandhi was educated in law in London, and when he later worked as a legal adviser in South Africa, he found himself treated as a member of an inferior race. Dismayed at the extensive denial of civil liberties and political rights to Indian immigrants in South Africa, he dedicated himself to a lifelong struggle for rights for Indians. Gandhi, who was deeply devoted to prayer, fasting, and meditation, became the international symbol of an India freed from British domination. Gandhi's advocacy of nonviolence was his expression of a way of life implicit in his Hindu religion. On January 30, 1948, on his way to an evening prayer meeting, he was assassinated by a Hindu radical.

Theodor Seuss Geisel (1904 – 1991)

Theodor Seuss Geisel, better known to the world as Dr. Seuss, was born in Massachusetts. Seuss's mother often soothed her children to sleep by singing, and he credited her for his ability to create the rhymes for which he became so well-known. Geisel wrote and illustrated forty-four children's books, including such classics as *Green Eggs and Ham* and *How the Grinch Stole Christmas*. His honors include two Academy Awards, two Emmys, a Peabody award, and the Pulitzer Prize.

Kahlil Gibran (1883 – 1931)

Born in a mountainous area in northern Lebanon, Kahlil Gibran was an inspiring Lebanese-American philosophical essayist, novelist, mystical poet, and artist (he once studied with August Rodin). Gibran is best-known for *The Prophet,* a book of twenty-six poetic essays published in 1923, which has been translated into over twenty languages.

The Bhagavad Gita

The Bhagavad Gita (also referred to as The Gita) is an ancient Sanskrit text consisting of seven hundred verses of the Mahabharata, a major Sanskrit epic of ancient India. The Gita's verses are very poetic, hence its title, which translates to "the Song of the Divine One." Often described as a concise guide to Hindu philosophy, the Gita is considered sacred by the majority of Hindu traditions, and especially so by followers of Krishna.

Marshall Govindan (Unknown)

Marshall Govindan is best-known for his book *Babaji and the 18 Siddha Kriya Yoga Tradition*. Govindan gathered material for this book for about two decades after his initiation into Kriya Yoga techniques at the International Babaji Yoga Sangam Centre in Los Angeles in 1970. In 1989 he was inspired by the great master of Kriya yoga, Mahavatar Babaji, to write this book to introduce to the world the 18 Siddha Yoga traditions.

The Dalai Lama Tenzin Gyatso (1935 –)

The Dalai Lama is the head of state and spiritual leader of the Tibetan people. Born Lhamo Dhondrub to a peasant family, His Holiness was recognized at the age of two, in accordance with Tibetan tradition, as the reincarnation of his predecessor, the thirteenth Dalai Lama. Exiled from his native country by China's takeover of Tibet in 1959, the Dalai Lama has since lived in India and initiated a series of journeys that have taken him to some forty-six nations, where he has advocated religious tolerance and political freedom. He was awarded the Nobel Peace Prize in 1989 for his efforts to liberate Tibet using nonviolent methods.

Hafiz (Shamsuddin Muhammad) (Unknown)

Shamsuddin Muhammad, also known as Hafiz, is among the most beloved poets of Persia. He spent nearly his entire life in Shiraz, where he became a famous Sufi master. When he died in the fourteenth century, he was thought to have written an estimated five thousand poems, of which five hundred to seven hundred have survived. His *Divan* (collected poems) is a classic in the literature of Sufism. In 1923, Hazrat Inayat Khan, the Indian teacher often credited with bringing Sufism to the West, proclaimed that "the words of Hafiz have won every heart that listens."

Abraham Joshua Heschel (1907 – 1972)

Rabbi Abraham Joshua Heschel was a U.S. Jewish philosopher, considered by many to be one of the most significant Jewish theologians of the twentieth century. Born in Poland and educated in Germany, where he obtained his Ph.D. from Berlin University, Heschel taught at New York's Jewish Theological Seminary of America from 1946 to his untimely death in 1972.

He was also a great social justice advocate, an active leader in the U.S. civil rights movement, and a fighter for human rights internationally. He wrote many major works, including *Man Is Not Alone: A Philosophy of Religion* (1951), the companion volume *God in Search of Man: A Philosophy of Judaism* (1955), *The Prophets* (1962), and *A Passion for Truth* (1973). His books have been well-received by readers of the Christian religion and other faiths, playing a critical role in the Christian-Jewish dialogue. Rabbi Heschel reminded us: "Never forget that you can still do your share to redeem the world in spite of all absurdities and frustrations and disappointments." He also said: "A religious person is someone whose greatest passion is compassion and whose greatest strength is love, and defiance of despair. As a young person, I most admired a person's intelligence, and as I got older, what I admired the most was a person's kindness."

JESUS (6 B.C. – A.D. 33)

Over two billion people on earth currently follow the teachings and life example of Jesus as members of various Christian churches. Also known as Jesus Christ and Jesus of Nazareth (peace and blessings be upon him), Jesus was born in Bethlehem to Mary and grew up in Nazareth in Galilee. At the age of thirty, Jesus began his public ministry, which started when he was baptized in the Jordan river by John the Baptist (peace be upon him). Jesus then began preaching to large crowds, healing the ill and performing many miracles. He later chose twelve apostles to assist him in his mission to tell humanity about the coming of the kingdom of God, stressing redemption and commitment.

The Muslims believe Jesus was a great prophet and that his mother, Mary, gave virgin birth to him. Islam also believes in the miracles of Jesus and the Second Coming of Christ.

Almost all Christians believe that Jesus was crucified on the cross, that he arose three days later from the dead, and that he later ascended into Heaven with the promise that he would return in what is called the Second Coming of Christ. Christians and Muslims are enthusiastically praying for the return of Jesus (peace be upon him) and the peace, prosperity, and justice that he will bring with him.

HELEN ADAMS KELLER (1880 – 1968)

Helen Adams Keller was born a healthy child in Alabama, but at the age of nineteen months, she lost her hearing and vision because of illness. Against overwhelming odds and with the help of her dedicated teacher, Anne Sullivan, Helen grew into a highly intelligent and sensitive woman who wrote, spoke, and labored incessantly for the betterment of others. In 1964 Helen received the Presidential Medal of Freedom and in 1965 was one of twenty elected to the Women's Hall of Fame at the New York World's Fair.

PIR VILAYAT INAYAT KHAN (1916 –)

Pir Vilayat Inayat Khan was the head of the Sufi Order in the West (now named Sufi Order International) for many years before his recent retirement. Khan is a senior statesman of the world spiritual community and the author of several well-known books, including *Awakening: A Sufi Perspective*. He has traveled all over the world to teach and lecture on various topics that are common to all religions and humanistic philosophies. He has convened religious congresses in many countries, uniting religious leaders from many denominations.

DR. MARTIN LUTHER KING, JR. (1929 – 1968)

Dr. Martin Luther King, Jr., a Baptist minister from Atlanta, Georgia, was a leading figure in the American civil rights movement. His powerful lectures, dialogues, movements, and nonviolent marches sparked the conscience of a generation and a country deeply divided by racial tensions between Caucasians and African-Americans.

In 1955, inspired by the courage of Rosa Parks and the nonviolence advocated by Gandhi, King organized the boycott of the Montgomery, Alabama transit companies to force the desegregation of its buses. King's charismatic leadership inspired both America and the world, and in 1964 he was awarded the Nobel Peace Prize for his work on racial equality in the United States. Dr. King was assassinated in Tennessee on April 4, 1968.

SCHYAMA TSCHARAN LAHIRI (1828 – 1898)

Schyama Tscharan Lahiri, also known as Lahiri Mahasaya, was a direct disciple of the legendary yogi and Hindu saint Mahavatar Babaji. Mahasaya himself was Guru to Swami Sri Yukteswar, who in turn was the Guru of the famous Paramahansa Yogananda. Mahasaya is widely considered to have introduced to the Western world Kriya yoga, which teaches the correct balance between meditation and the fulfilment of worldly obligations.

LAO-TZU (CIRCA 300 – 500 B.C.)

Lao-Tzu was a sixth-century B.C. Chinese philosopher who is believed by many to be the founder of Taoism. A contemporary of Confucius, Tzu was searching for a way that would avoid the constant feudal warfare and other conflicts that disrupted society during his lifetime. The result was his book, *Tao Te Ching*, composed some time between the sixth and third centuries B.C.

GEORGE BURR LEONARD (1923 –)

George Leonard is a foremost pioneer and expert on human potentiality. He has written twelve books, including *The Transformation, Education and Ecstasy, The Silent Pulse, the Ultimate Athlete, The Way of Aikido,* and *Mastery.* He spent seventeen years as senior editor for *Look* magazine, during which time he covered the American civil rights movement, politics, and foreign affairs. Along with Esalen founder Michael Murphy, Leonard cofounded the Integral Transformative Practice (ITP), which attempts to integrate body, mind, heart, and soul.

JUDITH L. LIEF (UNKNOWN)

A Buddhist teacher for over twenty-five years, Judith Lief has written and lectured internationally on death, dying, and the application of mindfulness-awareness training. As one of the foremost students of meditation master Chögyam Trungpa Rinpoche, Lief is a well-known teacher in the Buddhist and Shambhala traditions and is the author of *Making Friends with Death: A Buddhist Guide to Encountering Mortality.* A former head of Naropa University in Boulder, Colorado, Lief is the executive editor of Vajradhatu Publications.

FRÉDÉRIC LIONEL (1908 – 1999)

Frédéric Lionel is known for his sensitive, thoughtful writings on consciousness, spirituality, and peace, in part shaped by his experiences in World War II. He was born in Geneva and established his own electronics technology company in Paris but lived, taught, and lectured throughout Europe and America. The product of a modern age, Lionel was able to meld authentic connections between spirituality and technology, philosophy and economics, natural science and religion, and Christianity and the mystical experience. His books include *The Magic Tarot: Vehicle of Eternal Wisdom* and *Revolution in Consciousness.*

HELEN M. LUKE (1904 – 1995)

Helen Luke studied psychological and spiritual issues throughout her life. A Jungian in the truest sense of the word, Luke helped many people explore their inner lives, grapple with life's greatest mysteries, and search for their true identities. Her many books include *The Way of Woman, The Laughter at the Heart of Things,* and *Old Age.* In the two years before her death, Luke conducted a series of filmed interviews that illuminated her own quite unusual life's journey.

NELSON MANDELA (1918 –)

Nelson Rolihlahla Mandela is a South African lawyer and worldwide human rights leader. Convicted of treason in 1961 for organizing the banned African National Congress, Mandela became a symbol of unity for the worldwide anti-apartheid movement during his twenty-seven years in prison. After his release in 1990, he became a powerful catalyst in forcing the South African government to abandon all apartheid laws. In May 1994, Mandela became the first democratically elected black president of the Republic of South Africa.

BOBBY MCFERRIN (1950 –)

Bobby McFerrin is a jazz-influenced, acappella vocal performer and conductor. His song "Don't Worry, Be Happy" was a number-one U.S. pop hit in 1988, although the phrase originated with the Indian guru Meher Baba in the 1960s. He has collaborated with many instrumental performers, including pianists Chick Corea, Herbi Hancock, and cellist Yo-Yo Ma. He is known for his four-octave vocal range and his ability to use his voice to create sound effects and in vocal percussion.

MUHAMMAD (A.D. 570 – A.D. 632)

The Prophet Muhammad (peace and blessings be upon him) was born in Bakka, Makkah (now Mecca in present-day Saudi Arabia). The Qur'an is said to have been revealed to Muhammad (peace be upon him) over a period of twenty-three years, from A.D. 610 to A.D. 632. Historical scholars universally agree that Muhammad (peace be upon him) was illiterate all of his life.

Western author and translator Thomas Cleary has done extensive research on Muhammad (peace be upon him). In his 1994 book, *The Wisdom of the Prophet: Sayings of Muhammad,* Cleary states, "Authentic accounts of the Prophet reveal him as a pragmatic man, down to earth yet brilliantly spiritual, stern in matters of right yet compassionate and clement, rich in dignity yet extremely modest and humble; a poignant storyteller gifted with a keen sense of humor, a manly and valorous warrior who was most kind and gentle with women and children; a diligent worker, a conscientious family man, a good neighbor, and a just [ruler].

"…Muhammad's call to prophecy did not come until he was forty years old, already a mature man with a distinguished reputation in the community. Popularly known by the epithets The True and The Trustworthy, Muhammad (peace be upon him) was not only an exemplary member of society, but also a profoundly spiritual individual who regularly took to contemplative retreat in a mountain cave outside the city [of Mecca].

"It was during such a retreat that revelation first came to him, through the archangel Gabriel, who embraced the Prophet in a powerful grip and told him, 'Recite! Recite in the name of your Lord, Who created: Who created humankind from a clot of blood. Recite, for your Lord is most generous, Who taught by the pen, taught humankind what it did not know.'"

ROBERT C. MUSSEHL (1936 –)

Robert C. Mussehl has practiced as a Seattle attorney for over thirty-five years, emphasizing plaintiff personal injury and medical negligence law. Mussehl actively participates in social justice and human rights issues on local, national, and international levels. In 1991, Mussehl founded Lawyers Helping Hungry Children, a nonprofit organization that has provided over three million meals to at-risk children, and he continues to work diligently to get similar campaigns initiated nationally.

Although Mussehl was baptized as an infant and was confirmed at the age of fourteen in the Catholic religion, he has been initiated as both a yogi (Self Realization Fellowship) and Sufi. Mussehl is a member of the Sufi Order International, North American Chapter, in addition to his Catholic religion. In 1991 he made a lifetime commitment to himself and to God to help feed impoverished, at-risk children both locally and globally.

DR. JAVAD NURBAKHSH (UNKNOWN)

Dr. Javad Nurbakhsh was born in Kerman, Iran. He attended medical school at the University of

Tehran and later became a professor and head of its psychiatry department until his retirement in 1977. Nurbakhsh was initiated into the Nimatullahi Sufi Path as an adolescent. By the age of twenty, he was appointed by his master, Munis Ali Shah, to the position of Sheikh (spiritual director), and after the death of Munis, Nurbakhsh became Master of the Nimatullahi Order at twenty-six. For more than fifty years, Nurbakhsh has written and edited numerous books on Sufism, clarifying its theory and practice.

ROSA MCCAULY PARKS (1913 – 2005)

In 1955, Rosa Parks was living in Montgomery, Alabama, a city with laws that strictly segregated Caucasians and African-Americans. When Parks refused to give up her seat on a city bus to a white man, she was arrested and fined. The subsequent bus boycott by African-Americans, led by Reverend Dr. Martin Luther King, Jr., caused a national sensation that eventually led to widespread desegregation in the United States and sparked the beginning of the civil rights movement of the 1960s. Parks became a national icon of civil rights and African-American pride and was awarded the Presidential Medal of Freedom in 1996 and a Congressional Gold Medal in 1999. When she died in 2005, she became the first woman in U.S. history to lie in honor in the U.S. Capitol Rotunda.

THE BOOK OF PROVERBS

The Book of Proverbs, in the Old Testament of the Bible, consists of a group of sayings that extoll wisdom, as well as longer, connected poems composed from the tenth to the fourth century B.C. The sayings are either statements that provoke further thought or are admonitions to behave in particular ways. The Book of Proverbs is conventionally attributed to Solomon as the prototype of Israelite wisdom, but many sages have had a hand in composing and collecting its subsections.

THE BOOK OF PSALMS

The Book of Psalms, in the Old Testament of the Bible, is an enormous collection of Hebrew religious poetry, consisting of roughly one-hundred-fifty pieces divided into five sections. Originally spoken or sung in various worship settings, the psalms were composed individually from the tenth through the fourth century B.C. and compiled in their present form by at least 200 B.C. Tradition assigns the psalms to King David, but titles to particular psalms also name Moses, Solomon, Ethan, Asaph, and the sons of Korah as authors.

THE QUR'AN

The Qur'an is the sacred book of Islam. It was revealed to Muhammad in the Arabic language, and it means "recitation." Muslims believe that God revealed the Qur'an to the Prophet Muhammad (peace be upon him) over a period of twenty-three years, between A.D. 610 and A.D. 632, and they consider it to be the last of God's revelations to humankind. Muhammad himself was illiterate, but his followers both memorized the revelations and wrote them down on parchments, stones, bones, sticks, and leaves.

Muslims believe that the Qur'an available today is the same as that revealed to Prophet Muhammad and by him to his followers, who memorized his words. Scholars accept that the current Qur'an was first compiled in writing by the third Caliph, Uthman ibn Affan, between A.D. 650 and A.D. 656. Affan sent copies of his version to various provinces of the new Muslim empire and directed that all variant copies be destroyed. However, some skeptics doubt the recorded oral traditions (hadith) on which the account is based and will say only that the Qur'an must have been compiled before A.D. 750.

From the beginning of the faith, Muslims believed that the Qur'an was perfect only as revealed in Arabic. Translations were the result of human effort and fallibility, as well as lacking the inspired poetry that believers find in the original Qur'an. Translations are, therefore, considered to be only commentaries on the Qur'an, or translations of its meaning, not the Qur'an itself.

JOHN DAVISON ROCKEFELLER, JR. (1874 – 1960)

John D. Rockefeller, Jr. is known as a philanthropist who gave more than $537 million to educational, religious, cultural, medical, and other charitable projects. He donated the land for the United Nations headquarters and helped create the Rockefeller Center in New York City. He is the son of John D. Rockefeller, who founded the Standard Oil Company.

PAT RODEGAST & JUDITH STANTON (UNKNOWN)

Pat Rodegast is a nationally known teacher and author who regularly channels a spiritual entity by the name of Emmanuel, who shares wisdom and insights on all aspects of life and death. Rodegast has written three books containing Emmanuel's messages about living and loving. Rodegast collaborated with Judith Stanton to write *Emmanuel's Book: A Manual For Living Comfortably In The Cosmos*, published in 1985.

RUMI (JALAL AD-DIN MUHAMMAD RUMI) (1207 – 1273)

Rumi was born in Balkh, a city that was then in the Persian province of Khorasan but is now in Afghanistan. Rumi was a worldwide-esteemed Sufi poet and mystic who lived and died in Turkey, where he founded the Mevlevi Order, also known as the world-famous "Whirling Dervishes." His major work was the *Mathnawi,* a twenty-seven-thousand-couplet poetic exposition of Sufi wisdom that expresses a combination of fables, scenes from everyday life, Qur'anic revelations, and metaphysics.

SIR WALTER SCOTT (1771 – 1832)

Born in Edinburgh, Scotland, Sir Walter Scott was a historic novelist and poet who in some ways can be considered the first author to be internationally known in his lifetime, with contemporary readers in Europe, North America, and Australia. A prolific writer, Scott created historical novels in a series called the Waverley Novels. His amiability, generosity, and modesty made him socially popular, and he was also famous for entertaining on a grand scale at his Scottish estate, Abbotsford.

SHEIKH MAHMUD SHABISTARI (1250 – 1320)

Sheikh Mahmud Shabistari was a famous mystic and poetic who spent most of his life in Tabriz, Iran. Tabriz was a capital of the new Mongol empire, and Shabistari's life was influenced by fierce doctrinal disputes stemming from a struggle between Christianity and Islam for the allegiance of the Mongol rulers. Because of the distressed status of the Muslim community, Shabistari, like many of his contemporaries, withdrew from the outer world and sought refuge in spirituality and mysticism. He is known for his masterfully written poem, *Gulshan-e-Raz,* or *Secret Rose Garden.*

JOTHI RAMALINGA SWAMIGAL (1823 – 1873)

Jothi Ramalinga Swamigal, also known as Vallalar, was born in Tamilnadu, India. He taught spirituality and established charitable institutions, such as the Dharma Salai feeding center and the Gyana Sabai (Seat of Eternal Wisdom). Swamigal is also considered one of the greatest Tamil poets of the nineteenth century, having composed thousands of verses celebrating universal love and peace, which are known as *Tiru-arut-Paa (Holy Poems Sweeter than Nectar)*.

THAKUR (SREE SREE THAKUR ANUKUL CHANDRA) (1888 – 1969)

Thakur was an Indian Hindu guru, physician, and founder of the Satsang ashram. He established schools, charitable hospitals, engineering workshops, a publishing house, and a printing press. Thakur, who served as a spiritual advisor to Mahatma Gandhi, was a prolific writer; noted among his ninety-four books are *Satyanusaran, Punyapunthi, Anushruti, Chalar Sathi, Shashvati,* and *Pritibinayak.*

THIRUMOOLAR (CIRCA 1,000 B.C. – 800 B.C.)

Thirumoolar, also known as Tirumular or Thirumular, is considered to be one of the greatest mystics in Indian history and one of the most renowned of the 18 Siddhas. He is traditionally said to have lived for three thousand years, but historians assign him to a period between 1,000 B.C. to 800 B.C. He composed three thousand verses in a spiritual encyclopedia known as *Thirumandiran (Sacred Mystic Words)*. His philosophy of immortality is found in many of his verses.

MARIANNE WILLIAMSON (1952 –)

Marianne Williamson is an internationally acclaimed spiritual lecturer and bestselling author, who has published nine books, four of which have been number-one *New York Times* bestsellers, including *A Return to Love* and *Everyday Grace*. Her books have been translated into numerous languages. She is the founder of The Peace Alliance, a grassroots campaign supporting legislation to establish a United States Department of Peace. She also founded Project Angel Food, a meals-on-wheels program for homebound people with AIDS in the Los Angeles area.

OPRAH WINFREY (1954 –)

Oprah Winfrey produces and hosts the award-winning TV talk show, *The Oprah Winfrey Show.* Her accomplishments as a television leader, producer, actor, magazine founder, educator, and philanthropist have established her as one of the most influential, respected, and admired public figures today. Winfrey has been named one of the 100 Most Influential People of both the twentieth and twenty-first centuries by *Time* magazine, one of only four people to achieve this honor.

SWAMI PARAMAHANSA YOGANANDA (1893 – 1952)

Born in Bengal, India, Paramahansa Yogananda is revered as one of the greatest spiritual figures of the twentieth century and also was one of the first to bring the art of Eastern yoga to the West. In his youth, Yogananda studied under the revered guru Swami Sri Yukteswar. In America, he founded the Self-Realization Fellowship, which continues his teachings about Indian yoga and meditation. He also lectured widely on spiritual themes, emphasizing that although other customs of religions may be different, their underlying principles are the same.

SWAMI SRI YUKTESWAR GIRI MAHARAJ (1855 – 1936)

Swami Sri Yukteswar was the guru to Paramahansa Yogananda and a direct disciple of Lahiri Mahasaya, who introduced him to Kriya yoga. Their intertwined lives are highlighted in Yogananda's famous book, *Autobiography of a Yogi*. In Yukteswar's book, *The Holy Science,* he suggests that all religions are bound by a common unity and one God, and his study of astronomy and science is also evident in the formulation of his Yoga theory. Throughout his life, Yukteswar spread the teachings and principles of Kriya yoga practice throughout the world and was noted for his extensive knowledge in Vedic astrology.

INDEX BY TITLE

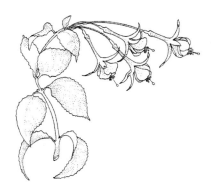

INDEX BY AUTHOR

INDEX BY FIRST LINE

ABOUT THE AUTHOR

ROBERT C. MUSSEHL

Robert C. Mussehl has practiced as a trial lawyer in Seattle for over thirty-five years, emphasizing plaintiff personal injury and medical negligence law. Mussehl actively participates in social justice and human rights issues on local, national, and international levels.

Mussehl was baptized as an infant and confirmed at the age of fourteen in the Catholic religion. In addition to his Catholic faith, he has been initiated as both a yogi (Self Realization Fellowship) and Sufi, and is a member of Sufi Order International, North America.

In 1980, he cofounded and chaired (1981 to 1982) the Washington State Bar Association World Peace Through Law Section. He served on the American Bar Association (ABA) Standing Committee on World Order Under Law for six years, serving as chair from 1986 to 1989, succeeding Father Robert Drinan, the previous chair (1983 to 1986), who recommended to the ABA president that Mr. Mussehl succeed Drinan as chair. This committee was responsible for spearheading challenging projects related to world peace and the protection of human rights, and sponsored numerous reform resolutions to the ABA House of Delegates for approval.

In 1991, Mussehl founded Lawyers Helping Hungry Children (LHHC), a nonprofit organization that has provided over three million meals to at-risk children, and he has chaired its campaign (1995 to 1997). He continues to work diligently to get similar campaigns initiated nationally. In 1997, for his work with LHHC, Mussehl was awarded the prestigious Jefferson Award, Washington State's highest award given in recognition for outstanding volunteer public and community service. In 1989, Father Drinan encouraged and inspired Mussehl to organize a hunger relief campaign with the support of lawyers, and LHHC was formed with Father Drinan's encouragement and blessings!

Mussehl has also made diversity a career-long priority. In 2004, the second African-American ABA president, Robert J. Grey, Jr., appointed Mussehl to serve as a commissioner on the ABA Commission on Racial and Ethnic Diversity. For the past three years, Mussehl has served as the editor of the ABA's *Goal IX* newsletter, which helps advance the role of minorities, women, and the handicapped in the legal profession and throughout the community at large.

Mussehl cofounded in 1991 and has served as chair of the ABA's Section of Dispute Resolution (2001 to 2002). He has been listed four times in *The Best Lawyers in America* and been regularly included in *Who's Who in America, Who's Who in American Law,* and *Who's Who in the World.*

Mussehl served as a member of the Interfaith Coalition for Human Rights, a Seattle-based organization of Christians, Jews, Muslims, Buddhists, and Hindus. From 1986 to 1988, Mussehl served as a member of the special ABA Blue Ribbon Committee on the World Court to study and consider a new acceptance by the United States of the compulsory jurisdiction of the International Court of Justice. This committee included former U.S. Secretary of State Cyrus R. Vance and several other leading world court experts. He has served on other interfaith and peace-seeking organizations, including a two-year term of office on the Board of Directors of the United Nations Association of the United States of America (Seattle chapter, 1989 to 1991). As both a human being and a lawyer, Mussehl's major career goal and life purpose is to promote and advance justice, interfaith harmony, and peace among *all* people of *all* faiths.

Mussehl is committed to work to the best of his God-given ability to attain the cherished ideal of "justice for all," which is the cornerstone of a free, peaceful, and prosperous world community. Mussehl believes that we *all* need to work hard together as an alliance to achieve pure, true, fair, and equitable justice.

He believes that Nelson Mandela has set a superb example of courageous leadership to emulate! Mussehl observes that Mandela has raised the bar for all of us when he declared to the world, upon taking the oath of office as the president of the Republic of South Africa, "Let there be justice for all, let there be peace for all, let freedom reign!" (See page 3 of the chapter entitled "Graceful Travels.")

Mussehl believes that we can enthusiastically choose to help Nelson Mandela, and other great heroes, social reformers, and advocates of social justice (like Abraham, Jesus, Muhammad [peace be upon them], Gandhi, Rosa Parks, Rabbi Abraham Heschel, Dr. Martin Luther King, Jr., Paul Findley, Father Robert F. Drinan, S.J., and Ammachi)* create their dream of a world community cemented by love, kindness, peace, freedom, and justice.

---

* Ammachi (better known as "Amma") deserves this recognition. Amma is a hero of Robert C. Mussehl, as a woman of great distinction and amazing accomplishments. (See her biography on page 168 and her website at www.amma.org.) She was recognized by the United Nations for her outstanding contributions to the world community and as an inspirational spiritual hero and leader.

PUBLICATIONS

AUTHOR

"Effective and Practical Family Law Negotiation." *Washington State Bar News* 38, no. 11 (1984). Article reprinted in *The Advocate, Idaho State Bar* 29, no. 3 (1986).

"Expanded Responsibilities of the Dissolution Lawyer." *Washington State Bar News* 36, no. 1 (1982).

"Washington Dissolution Practice: Meeting Divorce Clients' Needs." *Washington State Bar News* 33, no. 10 (1979).

"The Divorce Explosion: A New Role for the Lawyer." *Washington State Bar News* 31, no. 3 (1977).

"From Advocate to Counselor: The Emerging Role of the Family Law Practitioner." *The Gonzaga Law Review* 12, no. 3 (1977).

"Arbitration Could Bring World Peace to Our Troubled Planet." *Washington State Bar News* 31, no. 11 (1977).

"Arbitration of International Disputes." *Washington State Bar News* 30, no. 7 (1976).

"The Neighborhood Consumer Center: Relief for the Consumer at the Grass Roots Level." *Notre Dame Law Review* 47, no. 5 (1972).

COAUTHOR

"Law and the Hunger Crisis." *Washington State Bar News* 45, no. 5 (1991).

"Interstate Custody Disputes." *Washington State Bar News* 41, no. 11 (1987).

"Advancing the Rule of Law in the World." *Washington State Bar News* 39, no. 6 (1985).

Marvin v. Marvin. Parts 1 and 2. *Washington State Trial Lawyers Trial News* 16, no. 1 (1980); no. 2 (1980).

CONTRIBUTOR

Nader, Ralph, Lowell Dodge, and Ralf Hotchkiss. 1971. *What To Do With Your Bad Car: An Action Manual for Lemon Owners.* New York: Grossman Publishers. (Mussehl contributed sample letters and court pleadings that he had successfully used in pursuing the claim of a dissatisfied customer against a Seattle car dealer.)

Mussehl was a contributing writer from 1970 to 1973 to *The Consumer Advocate,* a periodical published by the ABA Consumer Affairs Committee (which was chaired by Mussehl), with a circulation of 5,000 persons directly involved in consumer affairs.

LEGAL PRECEDENTS

Marriage of Peters, 33 Wn. App. 48 (1982)

Mussehl successfully represented Dr. David L. Peters before the Washington State Court of Appeals, wherein the Appellate Court reversed the trial court's decision. This case established a new law in Washington by stating that a child support obligation may not be made subject to an escalation clause which operates automatically without regard to any changes in the noncustodial parent's income or other relevant circumstances. Mussehl argued that the 14th Amendment to the U.S. Constitution applied to this case under due process and equal protection provision Section 1, Amendment XIV (1886), the U.S. Constitution.

The court further stated that a child support award may not be based upon the noncustodial spouse's ability to pay without consideration being given to the contribution which the custodial spouse is able to make. Washington State child support guidelines were thereby substantially modified to include the income of the custodial spouse in calculating child support payments on a pro-rata basis.

United States v. Chapel, No. 24840, 428 F. 2d (1970)

Mussehl argued effectively before the United States Court of Appeals, Ninth Circuit, on June 29, 1970, to overturn a decision handed down by the United States District Court of the Western District of Washington, Northern Division, The Honorable William T. Beeks, Chief Trial Court Judge.

This precedent-setting case involved a young man who had been awarded a probationary period of three years after having been convicted for refusing induction into military service. Subsequent action was brought against the young man to revoke the probation as a punishment for having engaged in acts of civil protest against the Vietnam War. Mussehl presented an argument before the United States Court of Appeals which reversed the trial court's decision to revoke the probation. This was a landmark decision, limiting the discretionary powers of the federal trial court judge.

AMERICAN BAR ASSOCIATION (ABA) CONTRIBUTION

Chair, Special ABA Meeting with United Nations Secretary-General Javier Perez de Cuellar; his Under-Secretary-General; ABA President Robert MacCrate; and ABA Standing Committee members on World Order Under Law, including Hon. Edmund Muskie (former U.S. Secretary of State and U.S. Senator), Father Robert Drinan, and Paul Warnke (chief negotiator of the SALT II Treaty) at the United Nations, New York, N.Y., April 8, 1988, to discuss areas of mutual interest and concern including U.S. payment arrearages to the United Nations and the World Court Compulsory Jurisdiction.

Mussehl served twelve years (1979 to 1991) as a member of the ABA House of Delegates as a national Delegate-At-Large. The House of Delegates is the policy-making body of the American Bar Association. During his time as a Delegate-At-Large, Mussehl addressed the House of Delegates more than forty times in support of resolutions that promote world peace, human rights, social justice, access to justice, and the peaceful resolution of disputes.

In 1989, Mussehl signed a pledge with the ABA to make every reasonable effort to resolve conflicts through Alternative Dispute Resolution practices (ADR), such as negotiation, mediation, settlement conferences, mini-trials, and arbitration. The vast majority of Mussehl's cases are resolved through some form of ADR.

LEGAL AWARDS

In 1972, ABA President Chesterfield Smith presented two awards to Mussehl as immediate past chair of the King County Bar Association Young Lawyers' Section in recognition of the group's efforts in consumer protection, campaign disclosure law reform, human rights, protection of individual liberties, and combating drug abuse.

In 1995, Mussehl was nominated for both the Legal Foundation of Washington's Goldmark Award and the American Institute for Public Service's Jefferson Award for his tireless work on access to justice, especially social justice. In 1997, Mussehl was a recipient of the 1997 Jefferson Award, Washington State's highest award given in recognition for outstanding volunteer public and community service.

In 2000, Mussehl was selected and designated a "Quiet Hero" by the King County Bar Association.

ARTICLE REPRINTED FROM *SEATTLE POST-INTELLIGENCER*
FEBRUARY 2, 2005, BY CHERYL REID-SIMONS

2005 Jefferson Awards: For Lawyer, Social Justice Is At the Heart of Profession

Robert Mussehl is just the kind of guy to ruin lawyers' reputations.

That is, their reputations as defined by the countless jokes about greedy, soulless lawyers. Those jokes don't make the Seattle attorney laugh.

"We take an oath when we become lawyers that we're going to do our utmost to protect and preserve and make sure the justice system works," Mussehl said. "And it needs to work for everybody, or else nobody respects it."

To Mussehl, 68, practicing law isn't just another profession — it's a sacred trust and a way to serve society.

"All lawyers should feel that way," he said.

Maybe so, but not all lawyers take the notion of serving their communities to heart quite as much as Mussehl does.

As a founder and former director of the Washington State Lawyers Campaign for Hunger Relief — now known as Lawyers Helping Hungry Children — Mussehl's passion has helped to provide more than 3 million meals to help end the injustice of hunger.

His efforts on behalf of the state's hungry children earned him a Jefferson Award in 1997.

The Jefferson Awards, sponsored this year by the Seattle Post-Intelligencer *and The Boeing Co., have honored community involvement in Washington state for 28 years. The awards are named for Thomas Jefferson, the nation's third president, who drafted the Declaration of Independence and encouraged citizens to become involved in their communities.*

The P-I is accepting nominations for this year's awards. Any Washington resident can be nominated, including past nominees. The nomination form, an explanatory letter and supporting documents must be received by Feb. 11. A panel of community judges will choose five people among this year's nominees to be recognized at a ceremony March 18. One state winner will be selected to attend the national awards ceremony in Washington, D.C.

The awards were created in 1972 as a Nobel Prize for community service.

Mussehl said he was inspired to start a campaign to get lawyers involved in feeding hungry kids by one of his personal heroes in the legal profession, the Rev. Robert Drinan, a Catholic priest and law professor at Georgetown. "It was his dream to get lawyers involved."

Mussehl designed a model program, wrote a resolution, took it to the House of Delegates of the American Bar Association and the idea took off in several states.

When he brought it home to Washington, the state bar asked him to be in charge.

While no longer the director, Mussehl continues to serve on the board of the program he founded and is currently working on recruiting more lawyers to get involved.

He's also focused on increasing diversity in the legal profession. He serves on the Commission for Racial and Ethnic Diversity for the American Bar Association and has worked on diversity issues on the state and local levels, too.

In addition, he helped found the World Peace Through Law section of Washington's bar association.

It's all part of his idea of what it means to be a lawyer.

"I have just felt in my gut that social justice is the territory for lawyers," he said. "That's our realm and we need to make sure that the justice system works at all levels."

That's why he plans to keep working on peace and justice issues as long as he can.

"I'm going to do it until God decides to call me home," he said. "I don't want to retire."

ARTICLE REPRINTED FROM *WASHINGTON STATE BAR NEWS*, MARCH 2005

Seattle P-I *Article on 2005 Jefferson Awards Showcases Contributions of Seattle Lawyer Robert Mussehl*

A February 2, 2005, article in the Seattle Post-Intelligencer *titled "2005 Jefferson Awards: Social justice at heart of lawyer's profession" brings to light the remarkable contributions of Seattle lawyer Robert Mussehl to his community.*

"To Mussehl, 68, practicing law isn't just another profession," wrote the article's author, Cheryl Reid-Simons, "it's a sacred trust and a way to serve society." Mr. Mussehl is a founder and former director of the Washington State Lawyers Campaign for Hunger Relief — now called Lawyers Helping Hungry Children. In the article, Ms. Reid-Simons pointed out that "Mussehl's passion has helped to provide more than 3 million meals to help end the injustice of hunger."

That passion also earned Mr. Mussehl a prestigious Jefferson Award in 1997. Named for our third President and created in 1972 as a Nobel Prize for community service, the Jefferson Awards have honored community involvement in Washington state for the last 28 years.

Mr. Mussehl, who has been a member of the WSBA since 1967, continues to serve on the board of directors of Lawyers Helping Hungry Children, and is actively involved in recruiting additional lawyers. Also actively involved in promoting world peace and increasing diversity in the legal profession, he helped found the WSBA World Peace Through Law Section and serves on the ABA Commission for Racial and Ethnic Diversity.

God Bless You —
Always!